"FOR GALLANTRY
IN THE PERFORMANCE
OF MILITARY DUTY"

"FOR GALLANTRY IN THE PERFORMANCE OF MILITARY DUTY"

An account of the use of the Army Meritorious Service Medal to recognise Non-Combatant Gallantry 1916–1928

Major J. D. Sainsbury, t.d.

The Naval & Military Press Ltd

Published by

The Naval & Military Press Ltd
Unit 10 Ridgewood Industrial Park,
Uckfield, East Sussex,
TN22 5QE England

Tel: +44 (0) 1825 749494
Fax: +44 (0) 1825 765701

www.naval-military-press.com
www.nmarchive.com

In reprinting in facsimile from the original, any imperfections are inevitably reproduced and the quality may fall short of modern type and cartographic standards.

CONTENTS

		Page
Preface and Acknowledgements		7
PART		
I	Background Information	9
II	The Meritorious Service Medal "for Gallantry"	13
III	Bars to the Meritorious Service Medal	25
IV	Alphabetical List of Awards "for Gallantry" and Notes	27
V	Summary of Awards "for Gallantry" by date	55
VI	Awards "for Devotion to Duty"	57
VII	Bibliography	63

PREFACE

This short account of the use of the Army Meritorious Service Medal to recognise non-combatant gallantry has its origin in some detailed research on awards to the Bedfordshire Yeomanry during which I discovered the recommendation for Sergeant W. N. Owen (page 42). Further investigation showed how little was readily available on a little known aspect of a medal which would pass without second glance in a regimental museum display or on the chest of an old soldier. I hope these few pages will serve to place the Meritorious Service Medal "for Gallantry" in its rightful place in public esteem. My only regret is that in this materialistic age the detail that follows will, in addition to serving truth and historical record, further enhance the price (for value is no longer the right expression) of these scarce awards in a market which is all but unapproachable to regimental museums and other institutions whose role is to preserve our heritage without self-interest.

Although based principally on information published in the *London Gazette* or in *Army Orders* or available in the Public Record Office, this account is the richer for help I have received from officials and staff at the Ministry of Defence. In addition, Peter Abbott and John Tamplin have been most generous in sharing their knowledge of the Meritorious Service Medal, which they propose to include in any future revision of their unparalleled work *British Gallantry Awards*, and in patient discussion of detail.

As the manuscript was almost ready for the press I learned of the work which Ian McInnes had been carrying on over several years in order to provide readier access to information about the Meritorious Service Medal. After discussion on the overlap between our two books and the possibility of conflict, we concluded that this account, which throws part of his general survey into sharp focus should proceed independently.

As the text indicates, there are several facets of the complex story of awards for gallantry "not in the face of the enemy" which are inadequately recorded, and I hope to return to some of them in later publications.

Finally, this expression of acknowledgement would be incomplete without a word of thanks to the ladies at Leeds who typed a tricky manuscript both speedily and skilfully.

J. D. SAINSBURY

Digswell, Welwyn,
Hertfordshire.
December 1979

PART I

BACKGROUND INFORMATION

Awards for services in action available at the outbreak of war
At the start of the Great War in August 1914 the range of awards available to recognise gallant and distinguished service was, by modern standards, limited and to a great extent restricted to service actually on the field of battle. The Victoria Cross, confined to acts of the highest personal gallantry, was available for award to all ranks; the Distinguished Service Order was available for award to officers and its approximate equivalent, the Distinguished Conduct Medal, to other ranks; and all ranks could be mentioned in despatches. Additionally, officers of the rank of major or above could be appointed to or promoted in an appropriate order of chivalry.

Development of awards for services in action
The scale of operations during the war developed so fast and to such an extent that this limited range of awards quickly proved inadequate and it was greatly extended as the war progressed. The changes are traced in *A Review of New Orders, Decorations and Gallantry Medals instituted . . . during the War . . .* and, in so far as they concern awards for gallantry in action, are considered in detail in *British Gallantry Awards*. The changes included:

> The revision of the statutes of the Order of St. Michael and St. George to permit appointment of officers of the rank of major or above "for services during the present War" (January 1915);

> The institution of the Military Cross (December 1914) and bars for second and subsequent awards (August 1916);

> The institution of the Military Medal with bars for second and subsequent awards (March 1916); and

> The introduction of an emblem to be worn on the ribbon of the Victory Medal to denote a Mention in Despatches for services during the war (January 1920).

Thus by the end of the war, the range of awards for service on the battlefield could clearly be seen to ascend through four levels of distinction but showed some difference of treatment between various ranks. This structure has survived to the present time.

Institution of awards for services not in action
As the war progressed there was increasing concern that awards hitherto considered to be for the recognition of services in action with the enemy were being devalued by their use to recognise more general services "in the field"— interpreted to include service at headquarters and elsewhere behind the lines.

Recognition of this type of service and of other valuable services by officers, e.g., in depots and training centres and with Home Forces and garrisons not actually engaged, was not satisfactorily provided for until the institution of the Order of the British Empire in June 1917 and its eventual split into Military and Civil Divisions. Instructions were, however, issued from time to time attempting to restrict recommendations for the principal gallantry awards to the recognition of services in actual combat with the enemy. Meanwhile, provision was made in October 1916 for services by other ranks that could not properly be recognised by the Distinguished Conduct Medal or the Military Medal to be recognised by special awards of the Meritorious Service Medal (see below). Relatively little use was made of the Military Division of the Medal of the Order of the British Empire.

Awards for non-combatant gallantry available at the outbreak of war

There remained the question of the recognition of acts of gallantry performed by military personnel while on duty, but not in such circumstances as would qualify for the award of the honours normally reserved for services under fire.

At the outbreak of war there existed only the Albert Medal, in two classes, primarily civilian awards but available to the Armed Forces to recognise acts of the highest gallantry regardless of rank. The strictest scrutiny was exercised over recommendations of military personnel for the Albert Medal of either class, with a view to ensuring that it was used only to recognise acts of non-combatant gallantry which could be considered on a par with acts which would, in action, merit award of the Victoria Cross (see page 17). *Gallantry* lists 13 awards of the Albert Medal in Gold (prior to August 1917 the Albert Medal, First Class) and 87 awards of the Albert Medal (prior to August 1917 the Albert Medal, Second Class) to Army personnel for acts of gallantry performed during the war.

The only other official awards available at the outbreak of war were the Board of Trade Medals (in Silver and in Bronze) for Gallantry in Saving Life at Sea (the Sea Gallantry Medal) and the medal was indeed used to recognise gallantry by Army personnel, in practice usually when embarked in troopships and transports that were torpedoed or mined or met other hazards. *Gallantry* lists 29 awards of the Sea Gallantry Medal to Army personnel for services during the war (Silver—23; Bronze—6).

It must be added that mentions in despatches could be awarded for non-combatant gallantry. However, it is not possible to tell, except in the case of the despatches especially devoted to loss of or damage to ships at sea, the extent to which mentions in despatches were so used.

If neither the Albert Medal nor the Sea Gallantry Medal was applicable, recourse could be had to the awards of various recognised societies, notably those of the Royal Humane Society, whose medals were authorised to be worn in uniform. The Lifesaving Medal of the Order of St. John was also awarded, relatively infrequently, to Army personnel.

Development of awards for non-combatant gallantry

The inadequacy of the range of official awards was keenly felt relatively early in the war, as evidenced by the large number of acts of gallantry by both officers and other ranks which are recorded as not having reached the standard necessary for award of the Albert Medal. These were kept "on ice", to the increasing embarrassment of the authorities, it may be assumed, and steps were taken to identify or introduce a suitable award. Curiously, it was acceptable in the first instance to introduce an award applicable only to other ranks —the special award of the Meritorious Service Medal "for gallantry in the performance of military duty otherwise than in action", described fully below and introduced in October 1916. Comparable acts of gallantry by officers could not be recognised until the institution of the Order of the British Empire in June 1917. It took some time to decide that it was appropriate to use the Order to recognise gallantry and in the Birthday Honours List of June 1918 (*London Gazette,* 7th June 1918) 5 officers were appointed O.B.E. and 62 M.B.E. "for an act of gallantry not in the presence of the enemy". Some of these acts had been performed as early as 1915 and most can be identified as acts originally submitted for consideration for award of the Albert Medal.

At the same time the Medal of the Order of the British Empire became available to recognise acts of gallantry by other ranks and some 75 were gazetted between 11th June 1918 and 7th July 1920 "for services in connection with the War in which great courage or self-sacrifice have been displayed". The distinction between acts qualifying for the Medal of the Order of the British Empire and those qualifying for the Meritorious Service Medal is not clear and the evident duplication, particularly after the changes in the terms of award of the Medal of the Order of the British Empire in 1922, contributed to the decision to discontinue special awards of the Meritorious Service Medal in 1928.

Mention should also be made of changes in the statutes of the Edward Medal to permit awards to the troops involved in the disastrous explosion at Faversham in April 1916 (see *Journal of the Orders and Medals Research Society—* Summer 1979).

By the end of the war the range of awards, both official and approved unofficial, available to recognise gallantry "not in the face of the enemy" exceeded the range available for gallantry in action and was very much more complex. Indeed it has taken many years of further evolution to produce the present structure of Queen's Commendation for Brave Conduct, Queen's Gallantry Medal, George Medal and George Cross. While these awards ascend through four levels, as do those for gallantry in action, there is now no distinction based on the rank of the recipient and, unlike awards for services in action, all four may now be awarded posthumously.

PART II

THE MERITORIOUS SERVICE MEDAL "FOR GALLANTRY"

Origin of the Meritorious Service Medal

The Meritorious Service Medal was instituted in 1845. Award of the medal carried with it an annuity and its primary use has since been as a reward for long serving warrant- and non-commissioned officers of the Regular Army. There are instances of its early award to recognise gallantry in action (before the institution of the Distinguished Conduct Medal) and it has sometimes been awarded for gallantry not in the face of the enemy. A series of articles by J. M. A. Tamplin and others in the *Journal of the Orders and Medals Research Society* between 1973 and 1975 covers the origin and development of the Regular Army Meritorious Service Medal and refers to the introduction of a similar medal in both the Royal Navy and the Royal Air Force. This account covers only awards of the Army Meritorious Service Medal made in recognition of non-combatant gallantry under changes in the Royal Warrant effective between 1916 and 1928. No attempt has been made to cover the award in similar circumstances of the Royal Navy and Royal Air Force Meritorious Service Medals.

Changes in the Royal Warrant 1916

In October 1916 by Royal Warrant dated 4th October and published as Army Order 352 of 1916, the conditions of award of the Meritorious Service Medal were changed to enable the medal to be awarded to "warrant officers, non-commissioned officers and men who render valuable and meritorious service". Recipients of the medal under this additional clause would not normally qualify for payment of an annuity or gratuity as did recipients under the original conditions, which were not changed. In special circumstances, however, recommendations for sergeants and above could recommend that the recipient be registered for the annuity, but as this entailed joining a long waiting list it is doubtful if the additional award was of much practical significance.

News of the changes in conditions of award was telegraphed to Commanders-in-Chief in the field on 6th October 1916, as follows:

> "Authority is delegated to yourself and Corps Commanders if considered desirable, to award the Meritorious Service Medal without limit to all troops under commissioned rank for distinctly meritorious service or devotion to duty, not necessarily in the presence of the enemy, rendered in any theatre of war since August 1914. Indian Native Army is not eligible." (P.R.O. – W.O. 32/4958.)

Awards under the new conditions, but not those still being made under the original conditions, were announced in the *London Gazette* and the first list of awards was published on 18th October 1916.

Institution of a bar to the Meritorious Service Medal

Neither the Royal Warrant nor the telegram, which would have been the first news of the changes to reach the armies abroad, could be said to be explicitly drafted. Certainly, the medal had not at this stage specifically been made available to recognise gallantry and it is not clear whether any of the earliest awards were indeed for gallantry. However, an indication that its use to recognise gallantry was at least in the minds of those responsible for the changes in the Royal Warrant, is provided by the institution almost immediately of a bar to the Meritorious Service Medal. In response to an enquiry from the War Office the Private Secretary to the King replied on 13th October that His Majesty approved the institution of a bar "but only for additional acts of gallantry, not additional periods of meritorious service" (P.R.O.—W.O.32/4957). A further Royal Warrant dated 23rd November was accordingly published as Army Order 400 of 1916. It included the following:

> "It is OUR WILL AND PLEASURE and We do hereby ordain that anyone who, after having performed services for which the Meritorious Service Medal is awarded, subsequently performs an approved act of gallantry, not necessarily on active service, in the performance of military duty or in saving, or attempting to save, the life of an officer or soldier which, if he had not received the Meritorious Service Medal, would have entitled him to it, shall be awarded a bar to be attached on the riband by which the medal is suspended, and for every additional such act an additional bar may be awarded."

An attempt to clarify any inconsistency that might have arisen was made in December 1916 by War Office letter (68/Gen/2810/MS of 11th December). Theatre commanders were directed to restrict awards of the medal under the new conditions to:—

(i) Devotion to duty in a theatre of war;
(ii) Gallant conduct in the performance of military duty or in saving or attempting to save the life of an officer or soldier otherwise than in action.*

It was emphasised that the medal was not to be awarded for devotion to duty or gallant conduct in action. The bar was to be awarded for a second act of gallantry or for the first if the soldier already held the medal "for long and meritorious service" (P.R.O.—W.O.32/4958 and 5400).

Further Royal Warrant—1917

These instructions failed to give complete clarification and, indeed, implied that the bar was not available for award to soldiers who performed an act of gallantry but held the medal under the 1916 revisions for devotion to duty. In a further attempt to resolve doubt a new Royal Warrant dated 3rd January 1917 was published as Army Order 45 of 1917. As this was the enabling warrant

---

* It should be noted that while services leading to an award for devotion to duty must have been performed in a theatre of war, the medal could be and indeed was, awarded for gallantry at home or in garrisons abroad which were under substantially peacetime conditions. Furthermore, the medal could not be awarded for gallantry in saving the lives of civilians if the soldier was off duty; in this case the awards of the lifesaving societies were held to be appropriate.

for the great majority of special awards of the Army Meritorious Service Medal, it is reproduced below in full, together with associated amendments to King's Regulations published as Army Order 47 of 1917.

Army Order 45 of 1917

GEORGE R.I.

WHEREAS by the Royal Warrant of the 19th December, 1845, a silver medal, entitled "The Meritorious Service Medal," was created to be awarded to serjeants who rendered distinguished or meritorious service, and by the Royal Warrant of the 10th June, 1884, was extended to all soldiers above the rank of corporal, and by Our Warrant of the 4th October, 1916, was extended to non-commissioned officers below the rank of serjeant and to men for valuable and meritorious service;

AND WHEREAS WE are desirous of extending the conditions under which this medal may be awarded;

IT IS OUR WILL AND PLEASURE and We do hereby ordain that the Meritorious Service Medal may be awarded to warrant officers, non-commissioned officers and men who are duly recommended for the grant in respect of gallant conduct in the performance of military duty otherwise than in action against the enemy, or in saving or attempting to save the life of an officer or soldier, or for devotion to duty in a theatre of war.

IT IS OUR FURTHER WILL AND PLEASURE that Our Warrant, dated the 1st December, 1914, governing the Pay, Appointment, Promotion and Non-effective Pay of Our Army shall be amended, with effect as from the 4th October, 1916, as follows:—

1. The following shall be *substituted* for Article 1157:—

1157. An additional pension of 6*d*. a day for Europeans and 3*d*. a day for non-Europeans referred to in Article 1151, may be granted to a pensioner who is in possession of the Victoria Cross, the Military Cross, or the Medal for Distinguished Conduct in the Field, or the Meritorious Service Medal, if awarded in respect of gallant conduct and deemed to merit the additional pension.

2. The following shall be *substituted* for Article 1227:—

1227. A Silver Medal for "Meritorious Service" may be awarded to a soldier who fulfils the conditions laid down in the King's Regulations as regards valuable and meritorious service, or has been recommended for the medal on account of gallant conduct in the performance of military duty otherwise than in action, or in saving or attempting to save the life of an officer or soldier, or for devotion to duty in a theatre of war.

3. In Article 1228, 5th line, *for* "the medal for meritorious service" the following shall be *substituted*:—

"the Meritorious Service Medal, if granted for valuable and meritorious service".

4. Article 1229 shall be *cancelled*.

Given at Our Court at St. James's, this 3rd day of January, 1917, in the 7th year of Our Reign.

By His Majesty's Command,
DERBY.

Army Order 47 of 1917

King's Regulations—Amendments.

Meritorious Service Medal.

For the first 9 lines of paragraph 1747 *substitute*:—

1747. The form and time of recommendation for the grant of the Meritorious Service Medal depend on whether it relates to (*a*) devotion to duty in a theatre of war, or gallant conduct; or (*b*) valuable and meritorious service.

When recommended under (*a*) a full report should be rendered in duplicate to the War Office through the usual channels at the time of the occurrence. When recommending for gallantry, the G.O.C. should record his opinion whether the case merits the grant of the additional pension of 6*d*. a day, should the man ultimately be discharged with a pension. No other documents are required.

As regards (*b*) a recommendation for the medal in respect of valuable and meritorious service may be submitted only if the candidate has served for 21 years with the colours (except in the case of invalids, who may be recommended if discharged after 18 years' service), and if he has served in a regular unit. The annuity in respect of the medal is limited to ranks above that of corporal. The following instructions should be followed:—

(i) Recommendations should be in letter form, accompanied by certified copies of the conduct sheets and records of service on A.F. B 200. They should be forwarded direct to the War Office by the O.C. the regular unit to which the candidate belongs.

Paragraph 1747 *add* at the end:—

(vi) The possession of the medal for gallant conduct or devotion under (*a*) above does not qualify for the annuity; but a soldier above the rank of corporal holding the medal on that ground may be recommended for registration if and when he fulfils the other conditions required under (*b*).

Further steps to set and maintain standards for the award

At intervals during the Great War steps were taken to maintain the standards of various awards and to ensure that these standards were uniformly applied throughout the various theatres. Much of the effort was devoted to the awards for services in action and to achieving clearer definitions of such terms as "in the field" and "under fire", and steps to differentiate between awards for services in actual combat and other awards were suggested. A short account of the debate and the suggested outcome is given in *A Review of New Orders Decorations and Gallantry Medals instituted by His Majesty during the War* . . . and there is a range of contemporary papers in the Public Record Office (W.O. 32 especially 5232 and 5400). Generally these discussions had little effect on the award of the Meritorious Service Medal for Gallantry, though they produced further guidelines on the appropriateness of the Meritorious Service Medal for valuable services that had been rendered wholly or partly under fire (W.O. 32/4967).

It is of greater interest in considering the use of the Meritorious Service Medal to recognise gallantry to note steps taken to set and maintain the standard of the non-combatant gallantry awards. Papers at the Ministry of Defence record that "at a conference held in the Adjutant-General's room at the War

Office on 27th March 1917 upon the question of the award of the Albert Medal to serving officers and soldiers, the following decision was arrived at:

In consequence of the strongly expressed views of the Home Secretary as voiced by .... the Home Office representative to the effect that the Albert Medal is considered to be the equivalent of the Victoria Cross, its standard must not be lowered by its award for actions of a degree less than that which would merit consideration for the award of the latter decoration had the deed been performed in the presence of the enemy. It was decided that all recommendations for the award of the Albert Medal to serving officers and soldiers should be laid before the Victoria Cross Board who after consideration would forward the recommendation to the Home Secretary in cases where the deed of gallantry was considered to attain the Victoria Cross standard. In other cases where the degree of gallantry was not of the required standard the recommendations would in the case of warrant officers, non-commissioned officers and men be considered by the Military Secretary for the award of the Meritorious Service Medal and in the case of officers the recommendations would be refused."*

As a result of these deliberations the Adjutant-General's department were able to issue further, and by previous standards very comprehensive, guidelines on the awards available to recognise non-combatant gallantry. War Office letter 0137/4286 (A.G.10) dated 15th September 1917 was issued to Home Commands, Commanders-in-Chief in the Field and commanders of garrisons abroad on a scale sufficient for wide distribution (2,000 copies were printed). The letter is reproduced in full below:

SIR,

I am commanded to inform you that the Council have recently had under consideration a large number of recommendations for the award to officers and other ranks of the Albert Medal, the Edward Medal and the Meritorious Service Medal under Article 1227, Royal Warrant, as amended by Army Order 45 of 1917.

2. It appears to the Council that these recommendations show considerable want of uniformity as to standard, and that it is not generally understood that the Albert and the Edward Medals are only awarded for acts of gallantry of a very high standard equivalent, so far as it is possible to make a comparison, to those services which in the Field are considered worthy of the Victoria Cross.

3. No names will be considered for the Albert or Edward Medal unless the standard of gallantry is of such a nature as to attain to the level of acts of valour which, if performed on military service, merit the Victoria Cross. These considerations can only be comparative, and though the comparative services may be widely divergent, the elements of determination and bravery displayed, viewed generally in conjunction with the attendant circumstances, enables a comparison to be made.

Exceptional initiative or voluntary entrance into, or continued submission to exceptional dangers, are the outstanding features of acts which win the Victoria Cross—acts which have gone beyond obedience to the necessarily insistent demand of self-preservation—and unless equivalent elements exist in cases put forward for the Albert Medal or Edward Medal, recommendation can hardly be justified.

4. It does not appear desirable that the Albert Medal, the Edward Medal or the

---

* In practice most recommendations for awards to officers were held over for consideration for appointments in the Order of the British Empire (see p. 11).

Meritorious Service Medal, should be awarded for services which, though undoubtedly gallant, are in many instances inseparable from the responsibilities connected with the appointment of the individual and in respect of incidents at Bombing Schools in particular, there is a tendency for recommendations to become stereotyped.

5. When considering recommendations for the Albert Medal, the Edward Medal and the Meritorious Service Medal, the following conditions receive the close attention of the Army Council, viz.:—
- (a) The responsibilities of the individual, having regard to the duties of his appointment.
- (b) To what extent has the act or action gone beyond obedience to the instinct of self-preservation?
- (c) Would the act, had it been performed in the stress of battle, have attracted sufficient attention to justify recommendation for reward? In other words, is every officer or soldier who picks up and casts away an enemy unexploded bomb to be rewarded?

6. To exemplify (a) of the preceding paragraph, the duties of a fireman may be conveniently quoted as an analogous example. Like the instructor at a Bombing or other School where training is of a dangerous nature, he has constantly to face exceptional risks. Experience and expert knowledge, coupled with confidence in the manufacture of weapons or material, result in these risks not only being regarded in a far less formidable light, but also being in fact less formidable than would be the case if the risks had to be faced by an untrained man.

In regard to Bombing Instructors particularly, it must be borne in mind that little option remains for the instructor but to remove the source of danger as speedily as possible.

7. It is to be pointed out that for services of a gallant nature not in the presence of the enemy, the undermentioned forms of reward, other than promotion, present themselves.

(A) *Official Medals.*

(i) Albert Medal for saving life on land (two classes).

(ii) Edward Medal for saving life from mines and explosions where there is a danger of asphyxiation.

(iii) Albert Medal for saving life at sea (two classes).

(iv) Board of Trade Medals (silver and bronze) granted for saving life at sea in cases which are not of the standard required for the Albert Medal.

(v) Meritorious Service Medal, with additional pension.

(vi) Meritorious Service Medal.

(v) and (vi) are granted only to warrant officers, non-commissioned officers and men on account of gallant conduct in the performance of military duty otherwise than in action, or in saving lives of officers or soldiers.

(B) *Non-official Medals.*

(i) Royal Humane Society awards (silver and bronze medals, also Testimonials on Vellum and Parchment), granted for rescues and attempted rescues:—
- (a) From drowning in rivers, lakes, &c.
- (b) From dangerous cliffs.
- (c) At sea, in British, Indian and in Colonial waters where a Humane Society does not exist.
- (d) On the coast of the United Kingdom, in cases which do not come within the charter of the Royal National Lifeboat Institution.

(e) From asphyxia in mines, wells, sewers, &c.

(ii) The Stanhope gold medal granted by the Royal Humane Society, in addition to the above awards for the bravest act of the year.

(iii) The medals of the Royal National Lifeboat Institution (gold and silver).

NOTE—Any of the above non-official medals may be accepted and worn in addition to one of the official medals awarded in respect of a particular act of bravery.

8. The recommendation for a reward should not particularise the award unless there are outstanding features which render such a course desirable. In all cases, however, where the grant of the Meritorious Service Medal is applicable, it should be stated whether, in the event of that Medal being awarded, the grant of the additional pension is recommended.

9. I am to request that you will issue such instructions as may be considered necessary to ensure that due attention may be given to the points now brought to notice.

I am,
Sir,
Your obedient Servant,

....

In view of the remarks about bombing instructors' gallantry it is interesting to note the large number of early awards of the Meritorious Service Medal for Gallantry that arise from accidents during grenade practice. As no details of the actions leading to later awards are preserved (see page 22) it is not possible to tell whether recommending authorities accepted the advice.

Even so, the Adjutant-General's letter of 15th September 1917 was not the last word in the matter of special awards of the Meritorious Service Medal. Continuing debate about conditions of award of decorations for services in the field led to the issue on 10th August 1918 of instructions to clarify the distinction between services which qualifed for the Military Medal and those which were more suitably recognised by the Meritorious Service Medal (for Valuable Services rather than for gallantry). The Military Medal was to be awarded for a specific act of gallantry in action or for continuous gallantry over a specified period of active operations. The Meritorious Service Medal was to be awarded for valuable services and devotion to duty in the field, and if elements of gallantry, either immediate or sustained, were discernible the Military Medal was to be awarded instead. (P.R.O.—W.O.32/5400). As previously, much depended upon the interpretation of the spirit as well as the letter of the instructions.

Consolidating Warrant—1920

No further changes (other than the extension of awards for valuable services to Home Forces—see page 21) were made until well after all awards for the Great War had been settled. Some of the experience of the previous four years doubtless told in the wording of a new Royal Warrant dated 6th November 1920 and published in the *London Gazette* of 19th November. The new warrant consolidated the various changes and confirmed the availability of special awards of the Meritorious Service Medal despite the introduction of the Medal of the Order of the British Empire. The relevant clauses were as follows:—

"*Thirdly*—It is ordained—
(a) That the Meritorious Service Medal may be awarded to Warrant Officers Classes I and II, non-commissioned officers and men of Our Military Forces who are duly recommended for the medal by a Commander-in-Chief for gallant conduct in the performance of military duty (not necessarily on active service) or in saving or attempting to save the life of an officer or soldier, or for devotion to duty in a theatre of war.
(b) That a Commander-in-Chief when recommending a soldier of Our Military Forces for the Meritorious Service Medal (or for a bar to the same under (e) of this clause) for gallant conduct shall record his opinion whether the case merits the grant of an additional pension—6d. a day for Europeans, and 3d. a day for Non-Europeans—should the soldier be discharged with a pension;
(c) That the additional pension referred to in (b) of this clause may be awarded if the services are duly recommended by a Commander-in-Chief, and deemed to merit the additional pension; provided that this additional pension has not been previously awarded to the soldier;
(d) That in no circumstances shall the award of the Meritorious Service Medal for gallant conduct or devotion to duty carry with it any claim to the annuity granted under the second clause of this Our Royal Warrant;
(e) That should a soldier of any of Our Military Forces who has been awarded the Meritorious Service Medal (either with or without annuity) subsequently perform an approved act of gallantry (not necessarily on active service), in the performance of military duty or in saving or attempting to save the life of an officer or soldier, which, had he not already received the Meritorious Service Medal, would have rendered him eligible for it, may be awarded a Bar; and for every additional such act of gallantry an additional bar may be awarded.
(f) That any soldier of Our Regular Army who is granted the Meritorious Service Medal for gallant conduct or devotion to duty in accordance with the conditions laid down in this clause of this Our Royal Warrant shall, if subsequently recommended and approved for an annuity in accordance with the second clause of this Our Royal Warrant, receive the annuity only. In such case he will receive the annuity as well as any additional pension which may have been awarded him under (c) of this clause;
(g) That soldiers of an Allied or Associated Army, of ranks equivalent to those of Our Military Forces specified in (a) of this clause, who have been associated in operations with Our Military Forces, shall be eligible for the award of the Meritorious Service Medal, but no annuity or additional pension shall accompany such awards; and
(h) That a Register of the Recipients of the Meritorious Service Medal (and bars) awarded under this clause shall be kept in the office of Our Principal Secretary of State for War, but such Register shall be separate and distinct from the Register referred to under (d) of the second clause of this Our Royal Warrant.

Fourthly—It is ordained that the names of those upon whom WE may be pleased to confer the Meritorious Service Medal without annuity under the third clause of this Our Royal Warrant, shall be published in the *London Gazette*."

The award falls into disuse

Less than a dozen Meritorious Service Medals for Gallantry were to be awarded under the consolidating warrant. Indeed, the discussions leading to special awards being discontinued had probably started before the warrant was signed. The main factor in the argument against the continued use of the

Meritorious Service Medal to recognise gallantry was the change from the single Medal of the Order of the British Empire to the two Medals of the Order "for Gallantry" and "for Meritorious Service" by Royal Warrant of 29th December 1922. The Albert Medal remained the highest award for gallantry not in the face of the enemy. There followed the newly established Empire Gallantry Medal and then the British Empire Medal. Although the latter was described as "for Meritorious Service" it was frequently awarded for acts of gallantry that were not deemed to qualify for the higher awards. With greater attention focused on the recently instituted awards, very little use was made of the Meritorious Service Medal for Gallantry and only four more awards were made before a Royal Warrant of 7th September 1928, published in the *London Gazette* of 21st September revoked the Third and Fourth Clauses of the warrant of November 1920. Since then the Meritorious Service Medal has been used only for its original purpose, as a reward for long serving warrant officers and sergeants.

Gazette notifications

Special awards of the Meritorious Service Medal under the amending warrants of 1916 and 1917 were notified in the *London Gazette*, though it was not until the consolidating warrant of 1920 that this was formally required, while awards with annuity continued to be notified in regular lists issued with Army Orders. The *London Gazette* uses three preambles to lists of awards, differing occasionally in detail. After an introduction "His Majesty the King has been graciously pleased to approve the award of the Meritorious Service Medal to the undermentioned warrant officers, non-commissioned officers and men" the sentence concludes:

(i) "for valuable services"—often with an indication of the theatre of war or other details, e.g., "for valuable services with the Armies in France and Flanders", "for valuable services in Military Record Offices in the United Kingdom", etc.*

(ii) "for devotion to duty" (occasionally extended to "exceptional devotion to duty" or "exceptional devotion in the performance of military duties") —usually with an indication of the circumstances.

(iii) "for gallantry in the performance of military duty" (sometimes extended by "otherwise than in the presence of the enemy").

Awards "for valuable services"

This account is not concerned with awards under the heading "for valuable services", which constitute the great majority of special awards of the Meritorious Service Medal. Approximately 25,000 were made under War Office auspices between 1916 and 1928. Where details of recommendations have been preserved, as for example in unit or formation histories and in unpublished regimental

---

* The term "in connection with the War" is generally used to describe services in a non-combatant theatre, usually the United Kingdom. A limited number of medals were allocated to Home Forces between September 1918 and November 1919 without any change in the terms of the Royal Warrant (P.R.O. – W.O. 32/5399).

archives, it can sometimes be shown that there was devotion to duty under fire, but no instances are known of the "valuable services" heading being used to cover an award for a specific act of gallantry not in the face of the enemy. However, bearing in mind the confusion caused by the early warrants the possibility that some of the awards gazetted "for valuable services" between October 1916 and March 1917 are in fact in recognition of gallantry can by no means be ruled out.

Awards "for gallantry"

The first list of awards "for gallantry in the performance of military duty" was gazetted on 12th March 1917. Further lists appeared at frequent intervals, at least until all lists for War Services had been published. Altogether 435 awards of the Medal "for gallantry" were originated under War Office auspices and gazetted between 1917 and 1927. The gazette dates and breakdown between United Kingdom, Dominion and Colonial troops are shown in Part V. [For bars see pages 25 & 26.]

Citations

With only one exception—a list of awards for gallantry following the mining of a hospital ship—it was not until July 1920 that any form of citation accompanied the announcement of an award in the *London Gazette*. The very few awards gazetted between 13th July 1920 and 27th May 1927 have full citations but for all previous awards reference must be made to other sources if any indication of the circumstances of award is to be obtained.

The Ministry of Defence hold only an incomplete record of recommendations. As will be seen from the details given in Part IV. This record covers in full only awards gazetted on 12th March, 17th April and 26th April 1917, with occasional citations for awards gazetted up to 18th October 1917. Many of these recommendations are contained in a register of recommendations for the Albert Medal and can be identified as having failed to satisfy the conditions of the higher award. They were kept "on ice" until the Meritorious Service Medal became available to recognise acts of gallantry, and account for the bulk of the early gallantry lists.

Awards "for devotion to duty"

There appears to be some identifiable distinction between awards gazetted "for devotion to duty' and those "for valuable services". Where it is possible to distinguish the circumstances of awards for devotion to duty there is an underlying element of bravery, though usually over a much longer period of time than the split seconds often associated with awards "for gallant conduct". Accordingly all awards "for devotion to duty" have been listed in Part VI and the reader may draw his own conclusions on the basis of available information as to whether these awards should be included in an assessment of the use of the Meritorious Service Medal as a means of recognising gallantry.

Awards to Allied Forces

Special awards of the Army Meritorious Service Medal were made to appropriate ranks of the Allied Forces under the extensive arrangements for exchange of decorations in force during the Great War. At least 700 awards were made, with much the highest proportion going to the French Army. Records are incomplete and none have yet come to light which distinguish between awards for valuable services and those for gallantry. It may be assumed that there were very few, if any, of the latter. Awards to Allied Forces were not gazetted.

Description

Medal

There was no difference between the medals awarded with annuity and those awarded under the special provisions of the revised Royal Warrants of 1916–17. Throughout the period 1916–1928 the design of the Army Meritorious Service Medal did not change, although the fixed suspender replaced the swivelling version around 1926. The obverse and reverse of the medal awarded for gallantry to C.Q.M.S. W. J. Clements are shown on the cover. Awards made under War Office auspices to personnel administered by the Admiralty or the Air Ministry were of the Army-pattern medal.

All medals are impressed in sans serif capitals to show the recipient's number, rank, initials; name and regiment or corps. Many show exact details of the recipient's unit, e.g., B/345 BDE, R.F.A.

Bar

The narrow laurelled bar first minted for use with the Distinguished Conduct Medal in 1917 was used.

Ribbon

Under Army Order 133 of 1916 the ribbons of both the Long Service and Good Conduct Medal and the Meritorious Service Medal were ordered to be crimson with white edges. In July 1917 (Army Order 238 of 1917) a central white stripe was added to the ribbon of the Meritorious Service Medal so that the two ribbons could readily be distinguished. The ribbon is $1\frac{1}{4}$ inches (32 mm) wide with edges and central stripe of approximately $\frac{1}{8}$ inches (3 mm).

Precedence of the award

There is no difference in the order of wearing between Meritorious Service Medals for gallantry, other awards under the revised warrants and awards with annuity. All are worn after the Army Long Service and Good Conduct Medal and have been so worn since 1911. However, the order of wearing cannot in this case be taken as an indication of the precedence of the award. It is clear that when awarded for gallantry the Meritorious Service Medal ranks below the Albert Medal of either class and the Edward Medal and, making allowance for the specialised nature of the Edward Medal could be said, at least during the Great War, to be the third highest award for gallantry by soldiers not in the face of the enemy. Second World War and present day analogues would be the British Empire Medal and the Queen's Gallantry Medal, both standing third, following the George Cross and the George Medal.

Contrary to some old soldiers' tales, there has never been any authority or recognised practice for the use of the post-nominal letters M.S.M. in the Army, even when the Medal was awarded for gallantry.

PART III

BARS TO THE MERITORIOUS SERVICE MEDAL

It will be recalled that in sanctioning the introduction of a Bar to the Meritorious Service Medal the King had stipulated that it should be awarded "only for additional acts of gallantry, not additional periods of meritorious service". The Royal Warrant of 23rd November 1916 gave effect to the spirit of His Majesty's command by making bars available for acts of gallantry performed by those who already held the medal, whether in recognition of gallantry or of meritorious service. Of the total of seven bars awarded, two were for a second act of gallantry and four were for the first act of gallantry when the medal was already held for meritorious service. Details of these awards are as follows:

1. *Bars awarded for a second act of gallantry* *London Gazette*

   SHENTON, 240229 Sgt. A. Manchester R. Home 19 Nov. 1917
   [Medal *L.G.* 26 May 1917 as 240229, Sgt., 2nd/5th Bn. York and Lancaster Regiment. (See page 45)]

   CARMODY, 530 Cpl. T. J. 3 Sqn. Austr. F.C. 17 Jun. 1919
   [Medal *L.G.* 21 Aug. 1917 as 530 2nd Cl. A.M., 69 Sqn. Australian Flying Corps. (See page 29)]

2. *Bars awarded for an act of gallantry after the medal had been awarded for valuable services*

   BERESFORD, 8250 Sgt. J. 3rd Bn. K.R.R.C. Waziristan 18 Feb. 1921
   "For gallantry and devotion to duty on 11th March 1920 while serving with the Waziristan Force. During a heavy snow storm he remained on duty transmitting important messages when the remainder of the staff had collapsed from the effect of oil fumes, thereby keeping open the only possible means of communication at considerable risk to his health."
   [Medal *L.G.* 14 May 1920 as 8250, Sgt., 3rd Bn. K.R.R.C.—N.W. Frontier.]

   COLEMAN, M/19684 Sgt. T. J. R.A.S.C. Turkey 11 Jul. 1924
   "This n.c.o. was directly in charge of the British Fire Brigade at Constantinople and in this capacity has been present at about 200 fires during a period of 22 months. The gallantry and devotion to duty displayed by this n.c.o. have resulted in the prevention of great material destruction and in the saving of many lives. Regardless of danger he has invariably placed himself in the position from which he could best direct the work of the brigade and has on several occasions only escaped death by the closest margin."
   [Medal *L.G.* 16 Oct. 1919 as T2/10223, Cpl., R.A.S.C.—Italy.]

ORR, 27253 Sgt. J.   R.A.M.C.   France   13 Feb. 1917

"On the occasion of the train accident at Gezaincourt on 24th November 1916 he fought the flames without ceasing in his efforts to rescue the wounded. He showed great gallantry in endeavouring to raise a blazing mass of wreckage to extricate an injured man who was pinned down by heavy beams of timber across his legs."

[Medal *L.G.* 11th November 1916 as 27253, Sgt., 29 Cas. Clg. Stn., R.A.M.C —France.]

COXON, P/10969 Cpl. J.   M.M.P.   France   20 Oct. 1919

[Medal *L.G.* 18 Jan. 1919 as P/10969, Cpl., M.M.P.—France.]

Opinions differ on the seventh bar, awarded to H/270001 R.Q.M.S. J. Elliott, Northumberland Hussars in the *London Gazette* of 28th August 1918. The facts, so far as they can be ascertained, are these. Elliott's first award was gazetted without any of the usual preambles on 27th June 1918 with three others—Corporal A. Ashburn, Canadian Forces and Sub-Conductor R. W. Lewis and Sergeant A. C. Rodrigues of the Railway Corps, East African Force. There is good evidence that the preamble "for gallantry in the performance of military duty" should have accompanied this list. The list follows a list of awards of the Military Medal, as do most other lists of awards of the Meritorious Service Medal for Gallantry, and Lewis's and Rodrigues's awards were duplicated in a gallantry list in the *London Gazette* of 16th July 1918. Overwhelmingly, all four awards are recorded as "for gallantry" in Ministry of Defence records. While it may reasonably be accepted that Elliott's medal is for gallantry, greater difficulty arises in confirming the reason for the bar. It was gazetted under the preamble "in recognition of valuable services rendered with the Armies in the Field during the present War". It is difficult to place any other interpretation on this preamble and in the absence of any evidence to the contrary it may be supposed that this bar was indeed for valuable services, but its award did not contravene His Majesty's command since it was not for an *additional* period of meritorious service. Accordingly the seventh bar is included in this account as follows:

3. *Bar awarded for valuable services after the medal had been awarded for an act of gallantry*

ELLIOTT, H/270001 R.Q.M.S. J.   1st/1st North'd Hussars   France   28 Aug. 1918

[Medal *L.G.* 27 Jun. 1918 as H/270001, R.Q.M.S. 1st/1st North'd Hussars (See page 32)]

ALPHABETICAL LIST OF FIRST AWARDS OF

THE MERITORIOUS SERVICE MEDAL FOR GALLANTRY

Note: Unpublished recommendations are shown in square brackets.

For notes see pages 52 to 54.

Names of East and West African and Chinese personnel follow the main alphabetical list.

					London Gazette	Notes
AIRLIE	036091	Pte. E.	89 Coy., R.A.O.C.		20 Oct. 1919	1
ALDREN	243776	Pte. E. B.	5th Bn. Loyal R.	Home Forces	28 Sep. 1917	2
ALLEN	WR/266712	Spr. G.	Rly. Opg. Div., R.E.		7 Oct. 1918	
ALLPORT	200575	L.-Sgt. N.	4th Bn. North'd Fus.	France	13 Sep. 1918	3
ANDREWS	2567	Cpl. W. C.	32nd Austr. Inf. Bn.	France	17 Dec. 1917	
ANTHONY	MS/4312	Sgt. H. M.	R.A.S.C.	Ireland	22 Mar. 1920	
ASHBURN	444001	Cpl. A.	1 Can. Div. Empl. Coy.	France	27 Jun. 1918	
ASHLEY	685774	Bdr. C.	2nd/3rd W. Lancs. Bde., R.F.A.	Home Forces	12 Dec. 1917	4
ATKINS	280846	Pte. J. W.	1st/4th Bn. London R.	France	17 Sep. 1917	
AUSTIN	385402	Pte. J.	767 Area Empl. Coy., Lab. Corps	France	24 Jan. 1919	
BADGER	WR/252503	Sgt. B. R.	1 Broad Gauge Opg. Coy., R.E.	France	3 Jul. 1919	
BAILEY	200178	Cpl. S.	1st/4th Bn. R. Welsh Fus.	France	14 May 1919	
BAKER	49291	Sgt. B.	Special Bde., R.E.	France	17 Jun. 1919	
BAKEWELL	011233	S-Sgt. G. J.	89 Coy., R.A.O.C.		20 Oct. 1919	1
BANESTER	1175	Spr. S. G.	1st/4th Coy., Kent Fortress Engrs., R.E.	Home Forces	12 Mar. 1917	4
BARKER	17/601	Cpl. E.	17th Bn. North'd Fus.	France	25 Apr. 1918	
BARRY	695708	Sgt. G. P.	57 Div. Amn. Col., R.F.A.	France	17 Jun. 1919	
BATT	C/4337	Pte. A. J.	11th Bn. K.R.R.C.	France	9 Jul. 1917	
BAYNTON	L/41044	Gnr. C.	London Div. Amn. Col., R.F.A.		20 Oct. 1919	5
BEANEY	1085	Gnr. L. A.	2nd/1st Coy., Kent R.G.A.	Home Forces	12 Mar. 1917	4
BELL	7748	C.S.M. G., M.M.	32nd Bn. M.G. Corps	France	17 Jun. 1919	
BENNETT	53646	S.-Smith Sgt. A.	349 Siege Bty., R.G.A.		21 Oct. 1918	
BENSON	L/44974	Cpl. J. A.	41 Div. Amn. Col., R.F.A.	France	18 Jun. 1917	
BERRY	54793	Pte. O.	62 Gen. Hosp., R.A.M.C.	Italy	14 May 1919	
BERRY	305640	Gnr. R. O.	32 Bty., 8th Army Bde., Can. F.A.	France	24 Jan. 1919	
BIDDLECOMBE	5718378	Pte. A. W. W.	2nd Bn. Dorset R.	India	15 Mar. 1921	6

["For gallantry and devotion to duty during a fire at the arsenal at St. Thomas's Mount on the night of 18/19th June 1920. These soldiers were the first to undertake the removal of the bombs from the immediate vicinity of the flames, which they continued to do until ordered to rejoin the guard. The work was of a highly dangerous nature involving risk of explosion."]

Name	Number	Rank	Unit	Location	Date	Ref
BIGGS	685423	Bdr. H.	8 Div. Amn. Col., R.F.A.	France	20 Aug. 1919	7
BIGGS	1251546	Sgt. W. T.	Can. Rly. Tps.	France	17 Jun. 1919	
BIRD	M2/105620	Cpl. A. C.	177 Coy., A.S.C.	France	21 Aug. 1917	8
BLACKBURN	40120	Pte. B.	3rd Garr. Bn. L'pool R.	Home Forces	29 Aug. 1917	

["At Fishguard on 22nd April 1917 when seaplane N 1033 struck the cliff and burst into flames, Private Blackburn, at the risk of his own life, pulled the pilot out of the burning machine thereby saving him from being burned alive or blown up, for a few minutes afterwards, the bombs on the seaplane exploded."]

Name	Number	Rank	Unit	Location	Date	Ref
BONSER	654	Sgt. R. J.	1st Austr. Pioneer Bn.	France	11 May 1917	
BOWGEN	MI/5521	Sgt. E. H.	A.S.C.	Egypt	28 Jul. 1917	
BRACKEN	2900	Pte. B.	2nd Bn. Leinster R.	France	19 Nov. 1917	
BRADFORD	030239	Pte. A. H.	R.A.O.C.	France	24 Jan. 1919	
BRANNAN	10176	Pte. F.	104 Coy., M.G. Corps	France	10 Apr. 1918	9
BRENNAN	376389	Pte. A.	761 Area Empl. Coy., Lab. Corps	France	10 Apr. 1918	10
BROADHURST	129898	Sgt. V.	P Special Coy., R.E.	France	24 Jan. 1919	11
BROADHURST	66942	Sgt. W. F.	3 Indian Div. Amn. Col., R.F.A.	Egypt	3 Jul. 1919	
BROCKLESS	36708	Pte. J.	R.A.M.C., H.S. *Oxfordshire*	E. Africa	17 Sep. 1917	12

"For gallantry on the occasion of the mining of a hospital ship."

Name	Number	Rank	Unit	Location	Date	Ref
BROOKS	109166	Sgt. L. A. W.	Rly. Opg. Div., R.E.	France	29 Aug. 1917	13
BROWN	WR/550295	Cpl. W. R.	I.W.D., R.E.	Salonika	3 Jul. 1919	
BUNKER	280665	Pte. H.	1st/4th Bn. London R.	France	2 Nov. 1917	
BURGE	WR/175318	Spr. R.	4 Coy., Rly. Opg. Div., R.E.	France	24 Jan. 1919	
BUTCHER	223380	C.Q.M.S. N. A.	229 Div. Empl. Coy., Lab. Corps.	France	10 Apr. 1918	
CAIRNS	375	Spr. W. J.	E.M.M.B. Coy., Austr. Engrs.	France	17 Sep. 1917	14
CALDWELL	17093	Pte. F.	1st Bn. Loyal R.	France	26 May 1917	
CALLOWAY	593	Pte. W. D.	5th Bn. Austr. M.G. Corps		13 Sep. 1918	
CARGILL	1160	L.-Cpl. R.E.	10 Austr. Lt. T.M. Bty.	France	18 Jul. 1917	
CARMODY	530	2nd Cl. A.M. T. J.	69 Sqn., Austr. F.C.	Home Forces	21 Aug. 1917	15,16

["For gallant conduct in attempting to rescue the pilot from a burning machine."]

Name	Number	Rank	Unit	Location	Date	Ref
CARNELL	019235	Cpl. A. J.	89 Coy., R.A.O.C.		20 Oct. 1919	1

					London Gazette	Notes
CARPENTER	195044	Sgt. B. C.	20th Bn. Can. Inf. (1st Cen. Ontario R.)		21 Oct. 1918	17
CARR	386282	Pte. L.	1st/1st North'n Fd. Amb., R.A.M.C.		6 Aug. 1918	
CARTER	139227	Cpl. J.	183 Tunnelling Coy., R.E.		14 May 1919	
CATHERALL	WR/333070	Spr. C. H.	I.W.D., R.E.		17 Jun. 1919	18
CATHERWOOD	5063	Pte. F. R.	4th Austr. Div. Salvage Coy.	France	26 May 1917	19
CHAMBERLAIN	44916	L.-Cpl. J.	Rly. Opg. Div., R.E.		24 Jan. 1919	
CHAPMAN	WR/262256	2nd Cpl. W. W.	18 Lt. Rly. Coy., R.E.	France	17 Jun. 1919	20
CHARLESWORTH	638	S.M.T.	M.F.P.	France	18 Jun. 1917	
CHINN	P/1314	L.-Cpl. J. J.	M.F.P.	France	10 Apr. 1918	
CHISHOLM	418386	Cpl. G.	1 Corps Signal Coy., R.E.	Mesopotamia	17 Jun. 1919	
CHYMIST	L/9566	Sgt. F.	3rd Bn. Queen's R.	Home Forces	12 Mar. 1917	

["During live grenade throwing instruction, a bomb was dropped after the fuse had been lighted. Sergeant Chymist at once picked it up and threw it away, probably saving several lives by so doing." Sittingbourne, 3rd June 1916.]

CLARK	296391	L.-Bdr. F. J.	153 Hy. Bty., R.G.A.	Salonika	25 Apr. 1918	
CLARK	7134	L.-Cpl. W. H.	3rd Bn. R. Irish Rif.	Home Forces	12 Jun. 1918	
CLARKE	1729	Pte. S.	18th Bn. Durham L.I.	France	14 May 1919	
CLARKE	52267	Pte. S. J.	88 Coy., Lab. Corps	France	12 Jun. 1918	
CLAYTON	WR/274649	Spr. F. J.	54 Lt. Rly. Opg. Coy., R.E.	France	13 Sep. 1918	21
CLEE	574476	Pte. A. H.	883 Area Empl. Coy., Lab. Corps.	France	20 Oct. 1919	
CLEMENTS	3/7245	Pte. O. J.	3rd Bn. R. Irish R.	Egypt	25 Apr. 1918	
CLEMENTS	M/21380	C.Q.M.S. W. J.	11 Pontoon Park, A.S.C.	France	12 Jun. 1918	22
CLIFFE	42690	Pte. F.	72 Coy., Lab. Corps		14 May 1919	
COCKBURN	S/43081	L.-Cpl. W.	1st Bn. Black Watch	France	10 Apr. 1918	
COCKER	41856	Sgt. F.	1st Bn. Sco. Rif.	France	10 Apr. 1918	
COMER	685909	Gnr. E.	2nd/3rd W. Lancs. Bde., R.F.A.	Home Forces	12 Dec. 1917	4
COOK	1523	B.Q.M.S. P. G.	R.G.A.		12 Jun. 1918	
COOPER	35699	Gnr. E.	86 Hy. Bty., R.G.A.	Turkey (P.o.W.)	29 Aug. 1917	
CORNISH	031675	2nd Cpl. F. G.	R.A.O.C.	Egypt	20 Oct. 1919	23

COSFORD	G/106864	Pte. G.	43rd Bn. R. Fus.	France	20 Aug. 1919	
COTTER	1105	Gnr. C. P.	1st/1st Coy, Kent R.G.A.	Home Forces	12 Mar. 1917	4
CREW	08056	Sgt. E. T.	A.O.C.	France	10 Apr. 1918	
CRITCHLEY	685900	Dvr. G.	2nd/3rd W. Lancs. Bde., R.F.A.	Home Forces	12 Dec. 1917	4
DALZELL	666	Sgt. A. G.	69 Sqn., Austr., F.C.	Home Forces	21 Aug. 1917	16

["For gallant conduct in attempting to rescue the pilot from a burning machine."]

DAUGHTON	487	Pte. R.	1st/4th Bn. Lincoln R.	France	2 Nov. 1917	
DAVIE	24483	Pte. R.	104 Coy., M.G. Corps	France	10 Apr. 1918	9
DEAMER	420913	Pte. R. A. J.	211 Empl. Coy., Lab. Corps	France	20 Aug. 1919	
DELAHAYE	910367	Sgt. F. T.	21 Reserve Bty., R.F.A.	Mesopotamia	3 Jul. 1919	
DENNIS	805259	S.-S.Cpl. J.	B Bty., 231 Bde., R.F.A.	France	13 Sep. 1918	
DERRICK	19652	L.-Cpl. G.	104 Coy., M.G. Corps	France	10 Apr. 1918	9
DESSEZ	264494	Pte. C. V.	Can. A.S.C.		14 May 1919	
DICKENS	290276	L.-Bdr. F.	545 Siege Bty., R.G.A.	France	3 Jul. 1919	24
DICKINSON	7812380	L.-Cpl. E. J.	R. Signals	Waziristan	15 Feb. 1927	

["On the afternoon of the 4th June 1926 at Damdil Post, North Waziristan, Lance-Corporal Dickinson noticed that the small arms ammunition magazine was on fire. Without hesitation he ran into the magazine and helped to remove several boxes of explosives to a safe distance. Lance-Corporal Dickinson was in no way concerned with the charge of the magazine but instantly gave his assistance at a time of great danger. By his gallant conduct he helped very materially to prevent a serious explosion and consequent loss of life."]

DIXON	200476	L.-Cpl. E.	4th Bn. Border R.		17 Apr. 1917

["During live bombing practice on 15th December 1916, one of the men struck Lance-Corporal Dixon's hand in the act of throwing his bomb. He lost hold of the bomb which fell to the ground. Lance-Corporal Dixon rushed forward at once, picked up the bomb and threw it over the parapet where it immediately exploded. But for his prompt action, a serious accident would have occurred."]

DONNINTHORNE	22178	Gnr. W. J.	57 Siege Bty., R.G.A.		17 Apr. 1917

["On 25th December 1916 an oil stove used for heating a cartridge dugout caught fire. Seeing the fire, Gunner Donnithorne entered the dugout and threw out the stove and some material which had become ignited. He then extinguished the fire, so saving the cartridges which, had they become ignited, would have caused a serious explosion."]

DOWN	13575	C.Q.M.S. J. W.	R.G.A.	Aden	24 Jan. 1919	25

				London Gazette	Notes
DOWNER	306086	Sgt. E. J.	7th Bn. Hampshire R.	Mesopotamia 20 Aug. 1919	
DOYLE	1748	Pte. M.	18 Fd. Amb., R.A.M.C.	France 17 Dec. 1917	
DRENNAN	240671	Cpl. D.	1st/5th Bn. R. Scots Fus.	Egypt 29 Aug. 1917	
DUGDALE	688305	Dvr. B.	2nd/3rd W. Lancs Bde., R.F.A.	Home Forces 12 Dec. 1917	4
DUGGAN	25239	Pte. M.	7th Bn. R. Irish R.	France 23 Feb. 1918	
DUGLASS	500386	Cpl. J.	2 Army Tps. Coy., Can. Engrs.	France 12 Jun. 1918	
DUNN	1874	Cpl. G.	10 Sqn., R.F.C.	France 12 Mar. 1917	26

["On the 30th July 1916 at the airfield at Château Warppe, France, after a rack had been removed from a machine, a phosphorous bomb fell to the floor and the fuse ignited. Corporal Dunn immediately rushed to the scene, seized the bomb and ran round the machine and into the open, a distance of about thirty yards. The bomb exploded as he threw it away. By his presence of mind and courage, Corporal Dunn prevented a most serious accident and loss of life."]

DURIE	330372	Pte. J.	1st/7th Bn. R. Scots	Egypt 25 Apr. 1918	27
EAGLESFIELD	240117	Sgt. W. J.	1st/6th Bn. L'pool R.	France 26 May 1917	
EASTON	27241	Pte. G. H.	8th Bn. Yorkshire R.	France 2 Nov. 1917	
ECCLES	444312	Cpl. S.	42 Div. Sig. Coy., R.E.	France 11 May 1917	
EDWARDS	278	Bdr. A. F.	1st/1st Coy., Kent R.G.A.	Home Forces 12 Mar. 1917	4
EDWARDS	09984	Sgt. W. B. W.	R.A.O.C.	France 22 Nov. 1919	
EKINS	M2/099853	Pte. W. G.	141 Siege Bty. Amn. Col., R.A.S.C.	France 20 Oct. 1919	
ELLIOTT	H/270001	R.Q.M.S. J.	1st/1st North'd Hussars	France 27 Jun. 1918	28
ELLIS	247059	Dvr. P. C.	50 Div. Amn. Col., R.F.A.	France 14 May 1919	
ELLWOOD	74942	Pte. F. A.	51st (Grad.) Bn. L'pool R.	Home Forces 13 Mar. 1918	
ELVIN	7155	Pte. H.	7th Bn. Norfolk R. attd. 35 T.M. Bty.	France 11 May 1917	
ENGLAND	3266	Sgt. P. A.	3rd Bn. Br. West Indies R.	France 24 Jan. 1919	29
ENGLAND	8520	L.-Cpl. S.	1st Bn. Leics. R.	France 12 Mar. 1917	

["A party of men were cleaning bombs at a bomb factory in the trenches and one of them dropped the bomb he was cleaning. Corporal England who was with two other men in the bay heard the man shout 'Look out'. He dashed forward, picked up the smoking bomb and threw it over the parapet where it immediately burst. By his prompt action Corporal England undoubtedly averted a very serious accident." Ypres, 30th May 1916.]

Name	Number	Rank	Unit	Theatre	Date	No.
EPHGRAVE	G/21598	Pte. C. F.	1st Garr. Bn. E. Kent R.	Home Forces	28 Jul. 1917	30

["For an act of gallantry in rescuing an officer of the R.F.C. from a burning aeroplane."]

Name	Number	Rank	Unit	Theatre	Date	No.
ETCHELLS	380153	Pte. J.	25th Bn. L'pool R.		2 Nov. 1917	2
ETHELSTON	52221	Cpl. G. W.	88 Lab. Coy., R.E.	France	21 Aug. 1917	31
EVANS	8034	Sgt. E.	1st Bn. Shropshire L.I.		21 Oct. 1918	
EVERSHED	4673	Sgt. P.	3rd Bn. R. Sussex R.	Home Forces	12 Mar. 1917	

["During live grenade throwing instruction one of the class dropped his bomb. Sergeant Evershed immediately picked it up and threw it over the parapet. He had every opportunity of escaping danger himself and by his unselfish action probably saved the lives of several men who were unable to move." Newhaven, 17 October 1916.]

Name	Number	Rank	Unit	Theatre	Date	No.
EWART	376444	Cpl. D.	761 Area Empl. Coy., Lab. Corps	France	10 Apr. 1918	10
FEAKES	116107	Gnr. G.	260 Siege Bty., R.G.A.	Home Forces	28 Jul. 1917	
FERGUSON	1376	Sgt. W. G.	5th Bn. K.O.S.B.	Home Forces	12 Mar. 1917	

["While a party of bombers were practising throwing Mills grenades on 1st June 1916, a man threw his grenade too low. It struck the parapet and rolled back into the trench. Sergeant Ferguson grasped the grenade when it came within reach and threw it out of the trench where it exploded almost immediately."]

Name	Number	Rank	Unit	Theatre	Date	No.
FEVER	982	L.-Cpl. H. W.	1st/4th Coy., Kent Fortress Engrs., R.E.	Home Forces	12 Mar. 1917	4
FISHER	T/576	Arm'r. S.-Sgt. W. J.	R.A.O.C.		3 Jul. 1919	
FLOODGATE	44599	Bdr. J. J.	20 Div. Amn. Col., R.F.A.	France	17 Sep. 1917	
FOARD	145794	L.-Cpl. P. G.	R.E.	Egypt	20 Oct. 1919	23
FORD	WR/278556	L.-Cpl. W.	54 Lt. Rly. Opg. Coy., R.E.	France	13 Sep. 1918	21
FORRESTER	22008	Gnr. J.	39 Bty., 8th Bde., Austr. F.A.	France	14 May 1919	
FOXLEY	13765	Pte. J.	1st Garr. Bn. R. Warwicks R.	Egypt	25 Apr. 1918	
FREEMAN	23368	Pnr. H.	139 Army Tps. Coy., R.E.	Salonika	18 Jul. 1917	
FROST	L/9583	B.Q.M.S. F.	30 Div. Amn. Col., R.F.A.	France	17 Sep. 1917	
GAGE	M1/09180	C.Q.M.S. O.H.	A.S.C.	Egypt	28 Jul. 1917	
GALLAGHER	016237	Sgt. W.	R.A.O.C.	Iraq	15 Mar. 1921	32

["For gallantry and devotion to duty during a fire in an ammunition store shed at Basra on 3rd July 1919. These n.c.o.s by a total disregard of personal danger materially assisted in averting what might have proved a serious disaster by dismantling stacks and boxes of phosphorous and incendiary shells, some of which were actually burning. In spite of the fumes and risk of burns and explosion, they continued the work of removal until the bay of the store was cleared."]

					London Gazette	Notes
GARNER	164958	Spr. W. T.	518 Fd. Coy., R.E.	France	7 Oct. 1918	
GAULD	24/964	L.-Cpl. A.	4th Bn. North'd Fus.	France	13 Sep. 1918	3
GEARING	32802	Pte. D. L.	7th Bn. R. Fus.	Home Forces	28 Jul. 1917	30

["For an act of gallantry in rescuing an officer of the R.F.C. from a burning aeroplane."]

GEDDES	109543	Gnr. J. D.	11th Bn. Tk. Corps.	France	13 Sep. 1918	
GINN	890642	Bdr. J.	B Bty., 4th Res. Bde., R.F.A.	Home Forces	28 Jul. 1917	
GODDEN	06358	S.-Sgt. J. R.	R.A.O.C.		20 Oct. 1919	
GOLLAN	7501	Spr. T. H. B.	2 Tunnelling Coy., Austr. Engrs.	France	17 Jun. 1919	33
GOLLOP	5719524	Pte. F. W. G.	2nd Bn. Dorset R.	India	15 Mar. 1921	6

["For gallantry and devotion to duty during a fire at the arsenal at St. Thomas's Mount on the night of 18th/19th June 1920. These soldiers were the first to undertake the removal of the bombs from the immediate vicinity of the flames, which they continued to do until ordered to rejoin the guard. The work was of a highly dangerous nature involving risk of explosion."]

GOODWIN	M2/191767	Sgt. P. C.	R.A.S.C. (M.T.) att'd 545 Siege Bty., R.G.A.	France	3 Jul. 1919	24
GORE	WR/176316	Spr. H.	54 Lt. Rly. Opg. Coy., R.E.	France	13 Sep. 1918	21
GOULD	03308	Sub-Condr. W. H.	R.A.O.C.	France	18 Dec. 1919	
GOULDING	342996	L.-Cpl. J., D.C.M.	54 Lt. Rly. Opg. Coy., R.E.	France	13 Sep. 1918	21
GRAINGER	240723	Pte. W. H.	1st/5th Bn. R.W. Kent R.	Mesopotamia	17 Jun. 1919	
GREENGRASS	720442	Pte. E. J.	24th Bn. London R.	Russia	12 Dec. 1917	
GREY	44242	Fitter Cpl. G. J.	4 Bty., 7th Bde., R.F.A.	Baluchistan	15 Jan. 1920	
GRIFFITHS	56130	Sgt. W. H. T.	19th Can. Inf. Bn. att'd 2nd Can. Entrench'g. Bn.	France	17 Apr. 1917	

["A bomb with pin drawn was dropped in a bay adjoining that in which Sergeant Griffiths was on duty. With great courage he left his cover, picked up the bomb and threw it away one second before it exploded, saving an officer and man from almost certain death." Compigny, France.]

GRUBB	243623	Sgt. T. J.	1st Res. Garr. Bn. H.L.I.	Archangel	22 Jan. 1920	
GUYATT	2828	Pte. A. E.	4 Austr. Div. Salvage Coy.	France	26 May 1917	19

Name	Number	Rank	Unit	Location	Date	Notes
HALL	21812	Pte. F.	13th Bn. Durham L.I.	France	9 Jul. 1917	
HALL	WR/505660	C.S.M. G. A.	I.W.D., R.E.	France	7 Oct. 1918	
HAMMOND	03608	Sgt. C. W.	A.O.C.	France	19 Mar. 1918	
HAND	WR/250281	Cpl. J.	12 Coy, Rly. Opg. Div., R.E.	France	24 Jan. 1919	
HANLEY	509	Pte. H. A.	2nd Bn. Austr. M.G. Corps	France	20 Oct. 1919	
HANNA	67871	Dvr. H.	B Bty., 47th Bde., R.F.A.		6 Aug. 1918	
HARDING	H/13902	Pte. J. T.	13th Hussars	Mesopotamia	20 Oct. 1919	
HARDY	43137	1st Cl. A.M. J. I.	57 Sqn., R.A.F.		6 Aug. 1918	26, 35
HARPER	49213	Pte. G. E.	1st/7th Bn. R. Scots	Egypt	25 Apr. 1918	27
HARRIS	587	Sgt. C. T.	1st/4th Coy., Kent Fortress Engrs. R.E.,	Home Forces	12 Mar. 1917	4
HARRISON	132989	Bdr. H.	543 Siege Bty., R.G.A.	France	24 Jan. 1919	
HARRISON	81598	Gnr. J. H.	34 Bty., 189th Bde., R.F.A.	France	10 Apr. 1918	
HATHAWAY	4447	Pte. G.	5 Austr. Lt. T.M. Bty.		21 Oct. 1918	
HAWKES	036139	Pte. F. C.	R.A.O.C.	France	24 Jan. 1919	
HAWKES	269244	Pte. H.	1st/1st Bn. Herts. R. att'd Entrench'g Bn.	France	17 Apr. 1917	

["At Orillers on 1st March 1917 Private Hawkes performed an act of great gallantry while on a working party. He picked up a bomb after it had been fused by a blow from a pickaxe and threw it into a trench, thereby saving the lives of his comrades."]

Name	Number	Rank	Unit	Location	Date	Notes
HAYWARD	S4/245391	Cpl. A.	74 Div. Train, R.A.S.C.	France	3 Jul. 1919	
HAZELL	12053	L.-Sgt. R.	9th Bn. Cheshire R.	France	12 Jun. 1918	
HENDERSON	300424	L.-Sgt. J.	8th Bn. Durham L.I.	France	9 Jul. 1917	
HENRY	1960	Pte. A. L.	3rd Bn. Br. West Indies R.		24 Jan. 1919	29
HINDS	123323	Pte. A. H.	Depot Coy., M.G. Corps	France	6 Aug. 1918	
HINSON	S/16181	Pte. W. F.	R.A.S.C.	Italy	14 May 1919	
HOBBS	5144	Spr. C. F.	E.M.M.B. Coy., Austr. Engrs.	France	17 Sep. 1917	14
HOCKNEY	847	C.S.M. H. H.	59 Coy, Rly. Opg. Div., Austr. Engrs.	France	19 Mar. 1918	36
HOLBORN	X15	Cpl. J. S.	4th Bn. S. African Inf.	Home Forces	12 Mar. 1917	

["During live grenade throwing instruction a trainee threw a bomb which lodged in the parapet of the trench just above his head. Corporal Holborn pushed the man aside, grasped the bomb and threw it over the parapet, thus averting a most serious accident and probably saving several lives." Bordon, 23rd July 1916.]

						London Gazette	Notes
HOLLAND	5/106A	C.S.M.	J.	N.Z.A.S.C. att'd 2 Fd. Amb.	France	18 Jul. 1917	
HOLMAN	4/3416	Sgt.	W. H.	4th Bn. R. Sussex R.	Home Forces	12 Mar. 1917	

["During live grenade throwing instruction a grenade failed to clear the parapet. In attempting to get to the grenade the officer in charge slipped and fell just short of it. Sergeant Holman, although under cover of the traverse, immediately dashed forward, managed to pick up the grenade and threw it away, thereby averting what would have been a most serious accident." Broadwater Forest, 30th November 1916.]

HOLOHAN	5097	R.S.M.	T.	Leinster R. att'd West India R.	France	13 Sep. 1918	
HOMER	200489	Cpl.	A.	1st/4th Bn. Loyal R.	France	2 Nov. 1917	
HOLYWELL	354486	Spr.	R.	479 Fd. Coy., R.E.	France	17 Jun. 1919	37
HOOD	166	Pte.	G.	12th Bn. Yorkshire L.I.	France	17 Dec. 1917	38
HUGHES	102796	2nd. Cpl.	J.	175 Tunnelling Coy., R.E.	France	19 Mar. 1918	
HUNT	T2/SR/02284	S.S.M.	L. R.	A.S.C.		6 Aug. 1918	
HUNT	5/1194	Pte.	S.	5th Bn. R. Irish R.	Salonika	29 Aug. 1917	
HURST	09809	Sgt.	H. O.	XC Amn. Depot, A.O.C.	France	23 Feb. 1918	
HURST	168759	Dvr.	W. M.	London Div. Amn. Col., R.F.A.	France	20 Oct. 1919	5
HUTCHINGS	510313	2nd Cpl.	W.	R.E.	France	2 Apr. 1918	
IREDALE	36717	Pte.	E.	R.A.M.C., H.S. *Oxfordshire*	E. Africa	17 Sep. 1917	12

["For gallantry on the occasion of the mining of a hospital ship."]

JACKSON	L/46421	Dvr.	E.	104 Bty., 22nd Bde., R.F.A.	Italy	14 May 1919	
JACKSON	WR/506538	Spr.	F. S.	I.W.D., R.E.	France	12 Jun. 1918	
JACKSON	3012	Spr.	P. L.	59 Broad Gauge Opg. Coy., Austr. Engrs.	France	19 Mar. 1918	36
JACKSON	36719	Pte.	W.	R.A.M.C., H.S. *Oxfordshire*	E. Africa	17 Sep. 1917	12

["For gallantry on the occasion of the mining of a hospital ship."]

JACOBS	55436	Sgt.	W.	93 Lab. Coy., R.E.	France	29 Aug. 1917	
JAGGAR	1456	Cpl.	A.	12th Bn. Yorkshire L.I.	France	17 Dec. 1917	38
JAMES	022353	Pte.	V. G.	R.A.O.C.	France	18 Dec. 1919	
JEMISON	325026	Pte.	R.	9th Bn. Durham L.I.		7 Oct. 1918	

["For gallantry and devotion to duty during a fire in an ammunition store shed at Basra on 3rd July 1919. These n.c.o.s by a total disregard of personal danger materially assisted in averting what might have proved a serious disaster by dismantling stacks and boxes of phosphorous and incendiary shells, some of which were actually burning. In spite of the fumes and risk of burns and explosion, they continued the work of removal until the bay of the store was cleared."]

JEWITT	457839	Spr. F.	R. E.	Mesopotamia 17 Jun. 1919 39
JOHNSON	109830	Spr. J.	I.W.D, R.E.	Home Forces 12 Mar. 1917

["On 23rd August 1916, the tug H.S.7 was on a passage from Hull towing the barges Walker and City to Cardiff for shipment to Mesopotamia. When eight miles E.N.E. of Hartland Point in a heavy sea the tow rope broke. To secure the barges again it proved necessary to approach stern first and to avoid fouling the propeller. When near enough Sapper Johnson jumped aboard at great risk and managed with difficulty to secure a rope. Owing to the high sea running it was almost impossible to keep a footing but he nevertheless persevered with the dangerous task of hauling on board the ten inch tow rope. Whilst he was thus engaged and when the barge was only some ten feet away from the tug, a heavy sea struck her, causing her to list over at such an angle that Sapper Johnson lost his footing and was washed over the side. He saved himself by clutching at a rope but before he could pull himself back on board, another sea flung the barge against the stern of the tug. Sapper Johnson hung between the two and was terribly crushed, his left foot being completely severed above the ankle and his right foot smashed. He was secured and dragged on board the tug and received immediate first aid which in all probability saved his life. The barges had broken adrift twice previously and each time Sapper Johnson had boarded them showing great coolness, courage and pluck in the risky work."]

JOHNSTON	T4/245402	C.S.M. W. H., D.C.M.	4 Div. Train, R.A.S.C.	France 3 Jul. 1919
JOLLY	01385	S.-Sgt. T. W.	R.A.O.C.	France 24 Jan. 1919
JONES	355919	Sgt. A. M.	25th Bn. R. Welsh Fus.	France 3 Jul. 1919 40
JONES	023752	L.-Cpl. E. E.	A.O.C.	France 10 Apr. 1918
JONES	011968	S.Q.M.S. E. S.	R.A.O.C.	20 Oct. 1919
JONES	165579	Pte. G.	N. Som. Yeo. att'd 6th Dragoons	20 Oct. 1919
JONES	39623	Sgt. G. F.	2nd Bn. Worcs. R.	Egypt 12 Mar. 1917

["On 8th December 1916 whilst some men were sitting round a brazier in a hut, one of the men dropped something into the fire. Sergeant Jones saw the article to be a bomb and realising the danger he immediately tried to get it out of the brazier. After two attempts he succeeded in doing so and the bomb, thrown to the ground, immediately exploded. A number of men were slightly wounded but this prompt action probably averted a very serious accident."]

JONES	2309293	Sgmn. G. H.	R. Signals	Thrace 11 Jul. 1924

["On 28th November 1922 when patrolling a telegraph line in Thrace, he showed marked gallantry and devotion to duty in beating off single-handed two armed brigands."]

					London Gazette	Notes
JONES	M/15536	Pte. T. E.	R.A.S.C.	Egypt	29 Jul. 1921	

["At Kantara on 28th June 1920 during a train wreck on the Palestine Military Railway this soldier, though badly injured himself—one arm being practically useless—behaved in a most courageous manner, dragging the injured from the burning wreck. Being exhausted he fell insensible on the sand but on recovery continued to help carrying the injured to a place of safety."]

JORDAN	012783	Sub-Condr. E. W. G.	A.O.C.	France	13 Sep. 1918	
KEADLE	444893	Sgt. W. H.	82 Coy., Lab. Corps	France	29 Aug. 1918	
KEEFE	M2/073721	Pte. S. J.	49 Amn. Sub-Park, A.S.C.	France	2 Apr. 1918	
KING	9462	Sgt. E.	2nd (H.S.) Garr. Bn. E. Yorkshire R.	Home Forces	18 Jun. 1917	
KING	2124927	Cpl. J. R.	13 Lt. Rly. Opg. Coy., Can. Rly. Tps.		17 Jun. 1919	41
KISSACH	S/3612	Cpl. R.	3rd Res. Bn. Gordon Highrs	Home Forces	11 May 1917	
KRIEHN	G/31344	Pte. A.	Middx. R. att'd 1 Inf. Lab. Coy., Lab. Corps	France	6 Aug. 1918	42
LANCAKE	S/17951	Sgt. D.	13th Bn. Black Watch		20 Oct. 1919	
LANE	241247	Pte. J. R.	2nd/5th Bn. Loyal R.	France	18 Jun. 1917	
LARGE	85501	Pte. D. W.	143 Coy, Lab Corps	France	3 Jul. 1919	
LAWSON	6/10617	Sgt. A.	6th Bn. R. Irish Rif.		2 Nov. 1917	
LEE	630	1st Cl. A.M. C. M. T.	69 Sqn., Austr. F.C.	Home Forces	21 Aug. 1917	16

["For gallant conduct in attempting to rescue the pilot from a burning machine."]

LEONARD	14/18092	Cpl. J. B.	14th Bn. R. Irish Rif.	France	28 Jan. 1918	
LEWIS	16046	Sub-Condr. R. W.	Rly. Corps, E. African Force	E. Africa	27 Jun. 1918	43
LIDLOW	49715	Gnr. C. F.	R.G.A. att'd Z/1 T.M. Bty.	France	11 May 1917	
LILES	WR/278584	Spr. N.	54 Lt. Rly. Opg. Div., R.E.	France	13 Sep. 1918	21
LLOYD	011255	Sub-Condr. W. J.	R.A.O.C.	France	14 May 1919	
LOOMES	6526	Sgt. F.	5th Bn. K.R.R.C.	Home Forces	28 Sep. 1917	

["For an act of gallantry performed during grenade throwing instruction." 2nd June 1917.]

LOOSEMOORE	147039	Sgt. J. W.	P Special Coy., R.E.	France	24 Jan. 1919 11
LYGOE	25231	Pte. H. J. L.	167 Coy., M.G. Corps		12 Mar. 1917
MCAINSH	04215	Sgt. W.	R.A.O.C.	France	24 Jan. 1919
MCCAFFERTY	28217	Gnr. J.	85 Coy., R.G.A.	Aden	24 Jan. 1919 25
MCCANN	32532	S.-Sgt. J.	R.A. att'd S. & T. Corps, Ind. Army	Mesopotamia	27 Sep. 1920

["For gallant conduct and devotion to duty. He not only saved more than one man from dro wning but, after hours in the icy water, arranged for shelter and food for men and animals who were unable to cross to their lines."]

MCCULLOCH	624647	Spr. A.	8th Bn. Can. Rly. Tps.	France	13 Jul. 1920

["At Poperinghe on 12th August 1918 this man with two others assisted in detaching burning wagons from a train containing cylinders of poison gas and removing them to a place of safety. Despite the escaping gas the fire was ultimately extinguished, thereby averting a serious accident."]

MCCULLOCH	280107	L.-Cpl. A. G.	7th Bn. H.L.I. att'd Lt. T.M. Bty.	Egypt	25 Apr. 1918
MCCULLOCH	470359	Sgt. S.	528 (Durham) Fd. Coy., R.E.	Italy	14 May 1919
MACDONALD	3/5936	L.-Sgt. J.	1st Bn. Gordon Highrs		18 Jun. 1917
MCDONALD	266384	Sgt. R. S.	7th Bn. Scottish Rif. att'd 5th/6th Bn.	France	14 May 1919
MACGREGOR	108415	Pte. J.	Saskatchewan R., Can. Inf.		7 Oct. 1918
MCGUINNESS	6432	Pte. E.	5th Bn. Connaught Rangers att'd H.Q. 30th Div.		14 May 1919
MCKENNA	2125328	Spr. B.	13 Lt. Rly. Opg. Coy., Can. Rly. Tps.	France	17 Jun. 1919 41
MCKENZIE	P/2226	L.-Cpl. A.	M.F.P.	France	17 Sep. 1917
MCLEOD	3/6243	Sgt. A.	3rd Bn. Seaforth Highrs	Home Forces	12 Mar. 1917

["During live grenade throwing instruction one man struck the parapet with his grenade which rolled back into the trench. Sergeant McLeod who was behind the man at the time immediately picked up the grenade and threw it over the parapet. He undoubtedly saved several lives by so doing, as the grenade exploded in the air." Cromarty, 1st July 1916.]

MABBOTT	404	C.S.M. A.	8th Bn. Notts. and Derby R.	Home Forces	26 Apr. 1917

["On 29th January 1917 Sergeant Mabbott was in the observation post of a live grenade throwing range. Lieutenant Rover and Sergeant Ellis were in the throwing bay. Sergeant Ellis pulled out the pin of the bomb he was about to throw and let the lever fly off, retaining the bomb in his hand. Sergeant Mabbott, seeing the bomb was fused, ran round the observation post where he was himself in safety, with the object of getting Sergeant Ellis to throw the bomb. The bomb burst before he could reach Sergeant Ellis killing the latter and wounding Lieutenant Rover and Sergeant Mabbott. By going from the observation post to the throwing bay Sergeant Mabbott showed utter disregard for his own safety, his aim being to take the bomb from Sergeant Ellis in time to avoid a serious accident."]

				London Gazette	Notes
MACHIN	241688	Gnr. F.	23 Div. Amn. Col., R.F.A.	Italy	14 May 1919
MAHOOD	403482	Pte. G.	877 Area Empl. Coy., Lab. Corps		17 Jun. 1919
MAILE	269361	Spr. J.	10 Lt. Rly. Opg. Coy., R.E.	France	19 Mar. 1918
MALZER	G/35438	Pte. J.	Middx. R. att'd 1 Inf. Lab. Coy., Lab. Corps	France	6 Aug. 1918 42
MANSON	6034	L.-Cpl. H. M. O.	28th Bn. Austr. Inf.	France	10 Apr. 1918
MARCHINGTON	404884	L.-Cpl. H.	1 Tramways Coy., Can. Engrs.		14 May 1919 44
MASH	461	R.S.M. W. J.	16th Bn. Rifle Bde.	France	7 Oct. 1918
MATHERY	190	Pte. R. E.	12th Bn. Yorkshire L.I.	France	17 Dec. 1917 38
MATHESON	1022628	S.-Sgt. M. B.	Indian A.O.C.	India	27 May 1927

["On 6th April 1926 a fire broke out in a truck of explosives in Ferozepore Arsenal near the magazine. Staff-Sergeant Matheson knew that the truck contained explosives but in spite of this he entered the truck and immediately started to unload it and assisted in pouring water over the burning boxes of explosives. By his gallant conduct he helped to extinguish the fire and materially prevented a serious explosion and consequent loss of life."]

MATTHEWS	56722	Cpl. G. H.	R.E. att'd 95 Coy., Lab. Corps	France	14 May 1919
MATTHEWS	129716	Cpl. H. J.	72nd Can. Inf. Bn.		17 Sep. 1917 14
MAXFELD	176	Spr. H.	E.M.M.B. Coy., Austr. Engrs.	France	17 Sep. 1917 10
MAYBANK	376539	Sgt. J.	761 Area Empl. Coy., Lab. Corps	France	10 Apr. 1918
MAYLIA	17992	L.-Cpl. J.	13th Bn. Durham L.I. att'd 68 T.M. Bty.	Italy	29 Aug. 1918
MEADOWS	730541	Dvr. G. S.	267th Bde., R.F.A.	Egypt	12 Jun. 1918
MELVILLE	2627059	Spr. R.	13 Lt. Rly. Opg. Coy., Can. Rly. Tps.		17 Jun. 1919 41
MEREDITH	32966	Pte. F. S.	9th Bn. E. Surrey R. att'd A.O.C.	France	19 Mar. 1918
MERRITT	1078	1st Cl. A.M. A. J.	71 Sqn., Austr. F.C.	Home Forces	2 Nov. 1917

["For gallant conduct in attempting to save the pilot from a burning aeroplane which had fallen on the aerodrome on 5th July 1917, as a result of which he received severe injuries himself."]

MERRY	P/796	Cpl. T.	M.F.P.	Ireland	16 Jul. 1918
MILL	42174	Pte. A.	R.A.M.C. att'd 57 Sqn., R.A.F.	France	6 Aug. 1918 26, 35
MILLER	18582	2nd Cpl. H. A.	25 Army Tps. Coy., R.E.	France	12 Jun. 1918

MILLER	75820	R.S.M. R.	56th Bde., R.G.A.	France	14 May 1919
MILNE	P/12985	L.-Cpl. J.	M.F.P. att'd Marseilles Base L. of C. Area		17 Jun. 1919
MILNER	M2/132375	Pte. E.	1 Water Tank M.T. Coy., A.S.C.		7 Oct. 1918
MILWARD	443839	Sgt. E. B.	54th Can. Inf. Bn.	France	26 Apr. 1917

["During live bombing instruction Lieutenant Bromacombe, Sergeant Milward and a learner were in the throwing bay. The man under instruction hit the parapet with a live bomb and it fell back into the bay. Lieutenant Bromacombe and the man threw themselves flat but Sergeant Milward, who had the easiest means of escape, picked up the bomb and managed to throw it over the parapet just as it exploded, thus averting a serious accident." France, 23rd February 1917.]

MITCHELL	10139	Sgt. T.	1st Bn. R. Scots	Egypt	12 Mar. 1917

["During live grenade throwing instruction one of the class dropped his grenade after igniting the fuse. Sergeant Mitchell at once attempted to pick up the grenade but the man who had dropped it collided with him in his endeavours to get away and knocked the grenade from his hand. Sergeant Mitchell made a further attempt to pick up the grenade but it exploded before he could reach it, wounding him in the head." 30th March 1916.]

MONCRIEF	33089	Pte. R.	7th Bn. Wiltshire R. att'd H.Q. 79 Inf. Bde.		7 Oct. 1918
MOORE	05468	Cpl. J. T.	R.A.O.C.	France	22 Nov. 1919
MORRIS	017496	Sgt. W. J.	R.A.O.C.	France	20 Oct. 1919
MORRISON	2135	Pte. G. A.	1st Anzac Bn. Imp. Camel Corps	Egypt	6 Aug. 1918
NEILL	686271	Dvr. W.	2nd/3rd W. Lancs. Bde., R.F.A.	Home Forces	12 Dec. 1917
NEWTON	5437	Pte. M.	1st/5th Bn. R. Lancaster R.		17 Apr. 1917

["On 14th January whilst on regimental police duty at the guard room of C Camp, Private Newton showed great presence of mind and personal bravery. A fire broke out in the R.S.M.'s hut about fifty yards from the guard room and the hut was ablaze in a few minutes. Private Newton doubled across from the guard room with a fire bucket. On the way he met the provost sergeant whose clothing was on fire. He extinguished it by throwing the contents of the bucket over him and then ran on towards the hut. Here Private Newton found the R.S.M. with his clothing on fire rolling on the ground. He immediately took off his greatcoat and managed to extinguish the flames by wrapping it round the R.S.M. At this moment a shout was raised that there was another man inside the hut. Private Newton at once tried to enter the hut but could not do so immediately owing to the rush of flames coming through the door. He eventually got in and rescued a company sergeant major who was on the floor, dragging him into the open."]

NICOLSON	201099	Sgt. A.	2nd/4th Bn. Cameron Highrs	Home Forces	26 May 1917

					London Gazette	Notes
NICHOLSON	13333	Bdr. J. M.	R.G.A. att'd B Bty., A.-A. Group	France	26 May 1917	
NOBLE	151444	Gnr. H.	R.F.A. att'd B Corps M.T. Coy	France	7 Oct. 1918	
NORRIS	69380	2nd Cl. A.M. A. H.	47 Balloon Sect., R.F.C.	France	19 Nov. 1917	26
O'BRIEN	WR/175836	Spr. C.	54 Lt. Rly. Opg. Coy., R.E.	France	13 Sep. 1918	21
OGG	512385	L.-Cpl. W.	574 Army Tps. Coy., R.E.	France	21 Aug. 1917	
O'ROURKE	A/8009	Sgt. M.	3rd Bn. Scottish Rif.	Home Forces	10 Apr. 1918	
O'SHEA	12142	Flt.-Sgt. E. J.	2 Aeroplane Supply Depot, R.A.F.	France	29 Aug. 1918	26
OWEN	0/1702	Cpl. H. A.	A.O.C.	Egypt	12 Mar. 1917	

["While ammunition was being discharged from S.S. *Megantic* part of a hoist of 13-pr ammunition fell about forty feet into the bottom of the hold. Simultaneously there was an explosion and a vivid flash from below. Corporal Owen, with great courage, immediately lowered himself into the hold and managed to separate the burning ammunition from the remainder, which consisted of some thirty tons of 13-pr ammunition, half of which was high explosive. Corporal Owen remained in the hold until all danger was over, helping to direct the fire hose. But for his courage and promptitude the explosion would have had the most serious consequences for the ship and all on board." Alexandria, 24th–25th August 1916.]

OWEN	1975	Sgt. W. N.	3rd/1st Bedfordshire Yeo.	Home Forces	12 Mar. 1917	

["Whilst a party of men were being instructed in live grenade throwing one of the men hit the parapet and the grenade fell back into the trench. Sergeant Owen immediately seized it and managed to throw it over the parapet before it burst, his prompt action averting a very serious accident." Maresfield Park, 1st August 1916.]

PAGE	200046	Sgt. H.	2nd/5th Bn. W. Yorkshire R.	Home Forces	28 Sep. 1917	

["On 27th January 1916 at Larkhill a man throwing a live Mills bomb slipped on the firestep, knocked his elbow on the trench side and dropped the bomb, releasing the lever. Sergeant Page picked up the bomb and threw it over the parapet before it exploded."]

PALMER	614595	Pte. G.	30 Coy., Lab. Corps	France	3 Jul. 1919	
PAPILLON	3286320	Pte. J. B.	1 Coy., Can. War Graves Det.	France	11 Feb. 1920	
PARKE	2546	Sgt. W. F.	R.F.C.	Home Forces	17 Dec. 1917	26
PARKER	1366	L.-Cpl. S.	1st/4th Coy., Kent Fortress Engrs., R.E.	Home Forces	12 Mar. 1917	4

Name	Number	Rank	Unit	Location	Date	
PARKINSON	18/1083	Cpl. F.	20th Bn. W. Yorkshire R.	Home Forces	28 Sep. 1917	

["While throwing a live Mills grenade a trainee hit the parapet and the grenade fell back into the trench. Corporal Parkinson bent down and retrieved the grenade just in time to prevent a serious accident. This is the second occasion on which this n.c.o. has acted in this manner."]

Name	Number	Rank	Unit	Location	Date	
PARKINSON	19157	Dvr. W.	113th Bde., R.F.A.	France	21 Aug. 1917	
PEARCE	893	Gnr. A.	1st/1st Coy., Kent R.G.A.	Home Forces	12 Mar. 1917	4
PHILLIPS	T3/022488	Dvr. R. J.	18 Div. Train, R.A.S.C.		24 Jan. 1919	
PHILLISKIRK	54918	Cpl. T. G.	37 (Chinese) Coy., Lab. Corps		18 Dec. 1919	
PIMM	WR/29042	Spr. J. H.	323 Quarrying Coy., R.E.		17 Jun. 1919	
PLATTS	TR/5/84105	L.-Sgt. J.	91st Trg. Res. Bn.	Home Forces	12 Mar. 1917	

["During live grenade throwing instruction a grenade with lighted fuse was dropped. Corporal Platts at once rushed forward and, not having time to reach the bomb, knocked over the man who had dropped it and the officer in charge, falling on the latter and covering him with his body so that his feet covered the officer's head. The bomb exploded and Corporal Platts was wounded in the feet, so that but for his courage and self-sacrifice his officer would have been severely injured if not killed." Cramlington, 27th September 1916.]

Name	Number	Rank	Unit	Location	Date	
POLLARD	305631	Sgt. W. H.	1st/7th Bn. W. Riding R.	France	28 Jan. 1918	
POW	262494	Sgt. T.	R.E.	Mesopotamia	17 Jun. 1919	39
POWELL	7085	Cpl. R.	3rd Bn. R. Welsh Fus.	France	18 Oct. 1917	

["On 8th June 1917 Corporal Powell picked up a live grenade which one of the men had accidentally dropped into the trench, by his prompt action saving the life of the thrower."]

Name	Number	Rank	Unit	Location	Date	
PRATLEY	17493	Pte. T.	8th Bn. Gloucs. R.		14 May 1919	
PRICE	138253	Gnr. T.	120 Hy. Bty. R.G.A.		12 Mar. 1917	
PRICE	802	Cpl. W.	M.F.P.	Salonika	2 Nov. 1917	
PRIEST	624895	Gnr. G. M.	B Bty., 1st/1st H.A.C.	Egypt	28 Jul. 1917	
PYKE	25064	Spr. F. W.	5th Bn. Can. Rly. Tps.	France	3 Jul. 1919	45
RADBOURNE	2124811	Cpl. G. T.	58 Broad Gauge Opg. Coy., Can. Rly. Tps.		17 Jun. 1919	
RANKIN	3/7688	Pte. W.	6th Bn. Connaught Rgrs.	France	18 Jun. 1917	46
RANSTEAD	1522	Sgt. C.	2nd Bn. Rifle Bde.	France	2 Nov. 1917	
READ	M2/149072	C.S.M. E.	11 Pontoon Park, A.S.C.	France	12 Jun. 1918	22

					London Gazette	Notes
REECE	143934	Pte. T.	33rd Bn. M.G. Corps	France	14 May 1919	
REED	O/9378	Cpl. A. H.	R.A.O.C.		18 Dec. 1919	
REES	1042	Cpl. R. W. G.	1st/4th Coy., Kent Fortress Engrs., R.E.	Home Forces	12 Mar. 1917	
RICHARDS	010531	S.-Sgt. A.	R.A.O.C.	France	20 Oct. 1919	
RICHARDSON	79611	Sgt. J. E. L.	M.G. Corps (Motor)	Mesopotamia	3 Jul. 1919	47
RICHARDSON	387930	Spr. W.	479 Fd. Coy., R.E.	France	17 Jun. 1919	37
RICKETTS	T3/028055	Cpl. J. W.	30 Div. Train, A.S.C.	France	12 Mar. 1917	

["On the evening of 12th September 1916 the alarm was raised that a man was drowning in the La Bassée Canal. Corporal Ricketts ran sixty yards to the canal bank, removed his coat and dived in. With great difficulty he rescued the man who could not swim and had already sunk twice."]

RIDDLESWORTH	50184	Pte. H.	1st/4th Bn. Cheshire R.	Egypt	25 Apr. 1918	
RIDLEY	T3/026383	Dvr. N.	R.A.S.C. (H.T.) att'd 52 Fd. Amb., R.A.M.C.	France	24 Jan. 1919	48
RIGBY	MI/5529	Pte. H.	36 Div. M.T. Coy., R.A.S.C.		17 Jun. 1919	
RILEY	52546	Pte. W.	88 Lab. Coy., R.E.	France	21 Aug. 1917	31
RISE	MZ/130	A.B. F.	R.N.V.R., Drake Bn. R.N. Div.	France	17 Jun. 1919	49
ROBERTS	WR/508617	Sgt. H. J.	I.W.D., R.E.	France	14 May 1919	
ROBERTS	WR/552409	Spr. J. T.	I.W.D., R.E.	Black Sea	22 Nov. 1919	
ROBERTS	685805	Gnr. P.	2nd/3rd W. Lancs. Bde., R.F.A.	Home Forces	12 Dec. 1917	4
ROBERTSON	WR/270169	Spr. A. G.	18 Lt. Rly. Opg. Coy., R.E.	France	17 Jun. 1919	20
ROBSON	WR/269336	Cpl. A.	54 Lt. Rly. Opg. Coy., R.E.	France	13 Sep. 1918	21
RODRIGUES	16160	Sgt. A. C.	Railway Corps, E. African Force	E. Africa	27 Jun. 1918	43
ROGAN	2188411	Spr. J.	58 Broad Gauge Opg. Coy., Can. Engrs.	France	14 May 1919	
ROURKE	5291	Pte. J.	3rd Bn. Leinster R.	Egypt	25 Apr. 1918	
ROWE	201406	Pte. H.	2nd/4th Bn. York & Lancaster R.		28 Sep. 1917	
RYAN	3/7581	Pte. P.	6th Bn. Connaught Rgrs.	France	18 Jun. 1917	46
SANCTO	386108	L.-Cpl. H. E.	1st/1st North'd Fd. Amb., R.A.M.C.	France	6 Aug. 1918	17

SAVAGE	M1/09275	Cpl. W.	2 Amn. Sub-Park A.S.C.	France	18 Jul. 1917
SCOTT	10830	L.-Cpl. J. W.	4th Bn. North'd Fus.	France	13 Sep. 1918 3
SEABROOK	191704	Bdr. J. T.	P.A.-A. Bty., R.G.A.	France	13 Sep. 1918
SHELDON	10284	Pte. C.	7th Bn. N. Staffs. R.	Mesopotamia	20 Oct. 1919
SHENTON	240229	Sgt. A.	2nd/5th Bn. York & Lancaster R.	France	26 May 1917 15

["On 28th June 1916 during bomb throwing practice Sergeant Shenton saw a live bomb rebound into the trench, picked it up and threw it over the parapet. By his prompt action he saved a number of men from being killed or injured."]

SHEPHERD	5066	Sub-Condr. S.	A.O.C.	France	12 Mar. 1917

["At Caestres ammunition railhead on 14th August 1916 while ammunition was being unloaded and stacked a shell exploded, setting fire to an adjacent stack of ammunition. At the risk of his life, Staff-Sergeant Shepherd proceeded to stamp out the fire. Failing in this, with the assistance of some other men, he speedily extinguished the fire with buckets of water. The importance of his prompt action can be appreciated from the fact that the cartridges and boxes which were alight were burning right up against the stack on which the accident occurred and in close proximity to other large stacks of ammunition."]

SHERWIN	26528	Pte. W.	16th Bn. Notts. & Derby R. att'd A.O.C.	France	10 Apr. 1918
SHINN	M2/148712	Pte. J.	346 M.T. Coy., R.A.S.C.	Salonika	3 Jul. 1919
SIDEBOTTOM	36729	Pte. J.	R.A.M.C., H.S. *Oxfordshire*	E. Africa	17 Sep. 1917 12

["For gallantry on the occasion of the mining of a hospital ship."]

SIMONS	WR/503871	Spr. T.	I.W.D., R.E.	France	17 Jun. 1919 18
SIMPSON	75297	Pte. A. R.	B Bn., Hy. Branch, M.G. Corps	France	18 Jul. 1917
SKAE	115058	Cpl. J.	192 Coy., Lab. Corps	France	14 May 1919
SLINGSBY	5/627	C.S.M. T. W.	N.Z.A.S.C. att'd 1 Fd. Amb., R.A.M.C.	France	18 Jul. 1917
SMALLWOOD	21483	Sgt. H. G.	1st Bn. Ox. & Bucks. L.I.	Mesopotamia	20 Aug. 1919
SMITH	265385	Sgt. A. E.	1st/2nd Monmouth R.	France	17 Apr. 1917

["On 5th January 1917 during bombing practice an n.c.o. throwing a live bomb for the first time struck the back of the trench with his hand, thereby losing hold of the bomb which fell to the bottom of the trench. Sergeant Smith, in spite of being obstructed by the thrower, managed to get to the bomb, picked it up and threw it over the parapet where it immediately exploded. Sergeant Smith has served nearly 26 months in France and has been wounded."]

					London Gazette	Notes
SMITH	883	Cpl. G.	Austr. Provost Corps att'd H.Q. Anzac Mtd. Div.	Egypt	6 Aug. 1918	
SMITH	202566	Pte. G.	2nd/4th Bn. E. Yorkshire R.	Bermuda	21 Aug. 1917	
SMITH	G/64486	Sgt. H.	Depot, R.W. Surrey R.	Home Forces	23 Feb. 1918	
SMITH	2682	L.-Cpl. J. H.	1st/8th Bn. Middx. R.	France	12 Mar. 1917	

["On 21st July 1916 a party of men were unscrewing the cap of a bomb when the firing pin was heard to hit the percussion cap of the detonator. A man threw the bomb into an adjoining passage where 25,000 Mills bombs with detonators fitted were stored. Lance-Corporal Smith was sitting about four yards from the party. He realised the danger and fearing that the bomb would explode rushed up the passage and threw himself on to the bomb. As he did so the bomb exploded—wounding him all over the lower part of the body. He undoubtedly saved the other men from being wounded and the stored bombs from exploding."]

SMITH	79630	Sgt. J. J.	M.G. Corps (Motor)	Mesopotamia	3 Jul. 1919	47
SMITH	5/372	S.S.M. S. H.	N.Z.A.S.C. att'd 3 Fd. Amb., R.A.M.C.	France	18 Jul. 1917	
SMITH	684	1st Cl. A.M. V.	69 Sqn., Austr. F.C.	Home Forces	21 Aug. 1917	16

["For gallant conduct in attempting to rescue the pilot from a burning machine."]

SMITH	3303	Cpl. W. G.	5th Bn. Rifle Bde.	France	14 May 1919	
SMYTH	16/1039	Pte. D.	16th Bn. R. Irish Rif.	France	4 Feb. 1918	
SOUTHERN	612057	Pte. J. H.	39 P.o.W. Coy., Lab. Corps	France	20 Oct. 1919	
SPALDING	130452	Pte. F.	M.G. Corps Base Depot	France	17 Jun. 1919	
SPEEDIE	T2/017835	Dvr. A.	R.A.S.C. (H.T.) att'd 52 Fd. Amb., R.A.M.C.	France	24 Jan. 1919	48
SPEIGHT	12981	Sgt. A.	11th Bn. York & Lancaster R.	Home Forces	12 Mar. 1917	

["On 8th August 1916 during live grenade throwing practice a man accidently dropped his grenade after withdrawing the safety pin. Sergeant Speight saw what had occurred and although the fuse was well started picked up the grenade and threw it over the parapet. The party being instructed was composed of men who were throwing grenades for the first time and it is believed that this n.c.o.'s action prevented a panic and saved a serious accident."]

SPEIGHT	241191	Pte. B.	2nd/5th Bn. Yorkshire L.I.	France	29 Aug. 1917	

Name	Number	Rank	Unit	Location	Date	Page
SPENCE	870	Sgt. S. C.	59 Broad Gauge Opg. Coy., Austr. Engrs.	France	19 Mar. 1918	36
SPENCER	104122	Pte. E. J.	229 Fd. Amb., R.A.M.C.	Egypt	28 Jul. 1917	
STEED	Deal 8438	Sgt. B. L.	R. Marine Lab. Corps		20 Aug. 1919	49, 50
STEPHENS	356036	Pte. H. V.	25th Bn. R. Welsh Fus.	France	3 Jul. 1919	40
STEVENSON	320375	L.-Cpl. E.	15th (Suffolk Yeo.) Bn. Suffolk R.	Egypt	25 Apr. 1918	
STOKES	TR/4/150	Sgt. J.	57th Trg. Res. Bn.	Home Forces	12 Mar. 1917	

["During live grenade throwing instruction a badly thrown bomb lodged in the sod revetment on the inside of the throwing pit. With great presence of mind Sergeant Stokes immediately stepped forward, pulled out the bomb and threw it over the parapet, thus averting a serious accident." Kinmel Park Camp, 22nd November 1916.]

Name	Number	Rank	Unit	Location	Date	Page
STONE	13079	Sgt. N. P.	6th Bn. Dorset R.	France	28 Sep. 1917	

["On 21st February 1916 Sergeant Stone was instructing a squad of grenadiers at a Divisional Grenade School when one of the squad dropped a grenade into the trench after igniting the fuse. By his prompt and cool action Sergeant Stone undoubtedly saved the lives of several men.".]

Name	Number	Rank	Unit	Location	Date	Page
STONEHOUSE	1852006	Sgt. J.	R.E.	Iraq	28 Sep. 1921	

["For gallant conduct and devotion to duty on the occasion of a fire amongst motor lorries at Mosul on 28th June 1920. Although arriving late at the scene of the fire, this n.c.o. immediately became conspicuous by his disregard of danger and for his leading of the sappers. He immediately started to look round for new points from which the fire could be attacked. On several occasions he endeavoured to get into the back of one of the lorries to remove tins of petrol and other inflammable material which had not up till that time caught fire, but on each occasion he was driven back by the excessive heat. By his courage and example, he was responsible for getting the fire in this lorry under control."]

Name	Number	Rank	Unit	Location	Date	Page
SUNDERLAND	201381	Pte. E.	2nd/4th Bn. W. Yorkshire R.	France	18 Jun. 1917	
TASKER	388	Spr. F. A.	Can. Rly. Constr. Corps	France	14 May 1919	
TATUM	2497593	Spr. G. A.	7th Bn. Can. Rly. Tps.	France	2 Apr. 1918	
TAYLOR	036910	Pte. A. G.	116 Coy., R.A.O.C.	France	14 May 1919	
TAYLOR	G/19355	Pte. A. J.	1st (H.S.) Garr. Bn. E. Kent R.	Home Forces	28 Jul. 1917	30

["For an act of gallantry in rescuing an officer of the R.F.C. from a burning aeroplane."]

Name	Number	Rank	Unit	Location	Date	Page
TAYLOR	61393	Pte. H. B.	65 Fd. Amb., R.A.M.C.	France	28 Jan. 1918	
TAYLOR	29379	Pte. J.	1st Garr. Bn. Cheshire R.		7 Oct. 1918	
TAYLOR	235044	Pte. L.	10th Bn. W. Yorkshire R.	France	25 Apr. 1918	

					London Gazette	Notes
THEODORE	WR/510120	Spr. G.	I.W.D., R.E.	France	14 May 1919	
THIRKELL	16659	Tpr. H. S.	Austr. Lt. Horse Fd. Amb.	Egypt	16 Jul. 1918	
THOMAS	3779	Dvr. D. R.	8 Div. Amn. Col., R.F.A.	France	20 Aug. 1919	7
THOMAS	149746	L.-Cpl. W.	I.W.D., R.E.	France	19 Mar. 1918	
TIERNEY	200522	Pte. J.	1st/5th Bn. L'pool R.	France	14 May 1919	
TINCKLER	258281	Spr. H. T.	5th Bn. Can. Rly. Tps.	France	3 Jul. 1919	45
TOBITT	157473	Spr. S. P.	Rly. Opg. Div., R.E.	France	29 Aug. 1917	13
TODD	2536	Pte. A. R.	Austr. Cyclist Trg. Bn.	Home Forces	12 Mar. 1917	

["While a class was being instructed in live grenade throwing a grenade with lighted fuse attached was dropped. Corporal Todd immediately sprang forward, picked up the grenade and threw it over the parapet, where it immediately burst. But for his prompt action a very serious accident would have occurred." Chiseldon Camp, 3rd August 1916.]

TODD	TR/4/24119	Cpl. E. E.	63rd Trg. Res. Bn.	Home Forces	12 Mar. 1917	

"During live grenade throwing instruction one of the class hit the sandbags at the top of the trench and the grenade rolled back into four or five inches of mud. Corporal Todd immediately rushed to the grenade and with great difficulty picked it up and threw it over the parapet, his prompt action averting a serious accident." Kinmel Park Camp, 6th November 1916.

TOMEY	97093	C.S.M. H.	162 Coy., Lab Corps		20 Oct. 1919	
TREADAWAY	77725	Cpl. E.	R.F.C.	Home Forces	19 Mar. 1918	26, 51
TURNER		Sub-Condr. G. E.	Indian A.O.C.	India	25 May 1927	

["On 6th April 1926 a fire broke out in a truck of explosives in Ferozepore Arsenal near the magazine. Sub-Conductor Turner knew that the truck contained explosives but in spite of this he entered the truck and assisted to unload it. By his gallant conduct he helped to extinguish the fire and materially prevented a serious explosion and consequent loss of life."]

UNDERWOOD	4087	Spr. J. C.	2 Tunnelling Coy., Austr. Engrs.	France	17 Jun. 1919	33
VOYSEY	M2/082773	Cpl. C. E.	11 Pontoon Park, A.S.C.	France	12 Jun. 1918	22
WAGSTAFF	H/7641	Pte. F. H.	7th Hussars	Mesopotamia	20 Aug. 1919	
WALDRIN	80810	Pte. A. G.	135 Coy., Lab. Corps	France	24 Jan. 1919	
WALL	11089	Sgt. W.	11th Bn. W. Yorkshire R.	France	29 Aug. 1917	
WALLACE	853	C.S.M. A.	59 Broad Gauge Opg. Coy., Austr. Engrs.	France	19 Mar. 1918	

Name	Number	Rank	Unit	Location	Date	
WALSH	9265	Pte. M.	1st Bn. R. Irish R.	Salonika	18 Jul. 1917	
WALSH	369221	Pte. W.	778 Area Empl. Coy., Lab. Corps		17 Jun. 1919	
WALTERS	44776	Pte. H. J.	25th Bn. R. Welsh Fus.		3 Jul. 1919	40
WARK	2529326	Cpl. A.	13th Bn. Can. Rly. Tps.	France	3 Jul. 1919	
WARWICK	426333	Sgt. D. J. E.	E. Ontario R., Can. Inf.	France	15 Mar. 1921	52
WATSON	TR/4/24126	L.-Sgt. F. W.	63rd Trg. Res. Bn.	Home Forces	12 Mar. 1917	

["During live grenade throwing instruction one of the men failed to clear the parapet with his grenade which rolled back into four or five inches of mud in the bottom of the trench. Corporal Watson promptly picked up the grenade and threw it away, the grenade bursting practically as it left his hand." Kinmel Park Camp, 13th September 1916.]

Name	Number	Rank	Unit	Location	Date	
WEATHERLEY	390270	Sgt. W. H.	9th (Res.) Bn. London R.	France	28 Sep. 1917	
WEBB	139735	Spr. G. H.	151 Fd. Coy., R.E.	France	18 Dec. 1919	
WELLS	S/35601	Pte. J. R. A.	11th Bn. Rifle Bde.	France	10 Apr. 1918	
WHITE	120683	Sgt. H. G., M.M.	P Special Coy., R.E.		24 Jan. 1919	
WHITE	32287	Cpl. W. T.	85 Coy., R.G.A.	Aden	24 Jan. 1919	25
WHITEHEAD	71859	Pte. A.	175 Coy., Lab. Corps	France	22 Nov. 1919	
WHITFIELD	2/2296	Gnr. G. E.	N.Z.F.A. att'd Y.N.Z. T.M. Bty.	France	19 Mar. 1918	
WILKINSON	WR/264840	Spr. E. W.	64 Broad Gauge Opg. Coy., R.E.		17 Jun. 1919	
WILLIAMS	696080	Sgt. A.	57 Div. Amn. Col., R.F.A.		7 Oct. 1918	
WILLIAMS	G/19585	Pte. A.	1st (H.S.) Garr. Bn. E. Kent R.	Home Forces	28 Jul. 1917	30

["For an act of gallantry in rescuing an officer of the R.F.C. from a burning aeroplane."]

Name	Number	Rank	Unit	Location	Date	
WILLIAMS	266054	Sgt. A. E.	2nd/7th Bn. W. Yorkshire R.	Home Forces	28 Sep. 1917	

["On 7th February 1916 at Larkhill during the firing of improvised bombs from a Leach catapult a man who was lighting a fuse knocked a bomb out of the pocket of the catapult. Sergeant Williams immediately picked up the bomb and threw it clear of the trench where it exploded harmlessly."]

Name	Number	Rank	Unit	Location	Date	
WILLIAMS	1153	2nd Cpl. S. M.	1st/4th Coy. Kent Fortress Engrs., R.E.	Home Forces	12 Mar. 1917	4
WILLIAMSON	H/4163	Sgt. F. J.	8th Hussars		21 Oct. 1918	
WILLSON	27003	Sgt. W.	105 (Chinese) Lab. Coy., Lab. Corps	France	19 Mar. 1918	

					London Gazette	Notes
WILSON	104616	Sgt. C. E.	1 Tramways Coy., Can. Engrs.		14 May 1919	44
WILSON	775510	Cpl. W.	1st W. Riding Bde., R.F.A. att'd 49 Div. M.T. Coy., A.S.C.		7 Oct. 1918	
WOOD	90487	Pte. C. W.	15th (Glamorgan Yeo.) Bn. Welsh R.		14 May 1919	
WOOD	M2/270301	Cpl. F.	103 M.T. Coy., A.S.C.		25 Apr. 1918	
WOODFORD	2190	1st Cl. A.M. C. J.	R.F.C.	Egypt	19 Mar. 1918	26, 51
WOODWARD	25074	L.-Cpl. H. T.	1st Bn. R. Warwicks, R. att'd 10 T.M. Bty.	Home Forces	7 Oct. 1918	
WOOLRIDGE	17927	Farr. S.-Sgt. Z.	8 Div. Amn. Col., R.F.A.	France	20 Aug. 1919	7
WRIGHT	686377	Gnr. G. E.	2nd/3rd W. Lancs. Bde., R.F.A.	Home Forces	12 Dec. 1917	
WYPER	B/20051	Sgt. J. M.	1st Bn. H.L.I.	India	13 Jul. 1920	

["On 21st March 1918 during bombing practice at Bangalore, one of the officers was about to throw a bomb when he dropped it behind him. Sergeant Wyper, with great presence of mind, seized the bomb and threw it clear."]

YAXLEY	553653	Sgt. W. J.	60 (Chinese) Coy., Lab Corps.		18 Dec. 1919	
YOUNG	2604	L.-Cpl. A.	5th Bn. Loyal R.		12 Mar. 1917	

["On 17th August 1916 during live grenade throwing practice one of the men under instruction hit the parapet with a grenade which then fell into a box containing grenades at his feet. Lance-Corporal Young managed to get the grenade out of the box and over the parapet in time to avert an accident which it is considered would, most probably, have resulted in the loss of the lives of those in the trench." Oswestry, 17th August 1916.]

					London Gazette
East African Native Personnel					
Abdul Gadr Bilal	5989	L.-Cpl.	2nd/4th Bn. K.A.R.	E. Africa	24 Jan. 1919
Aboukir Ahmed	3715	Mulazim Sena	1st/4th Bn. K.A.R.	E. Africa	14 Jan. 1918
Bilal Mahabut	3554	Sgt.	1st/4th Bn. K.A.R.	E. Africa	18 Oct. 1917
Mohomed Bilal	5033	Pte.	2nd/4th Bn. K.A.R.	E. Africa	24 Jan. 1919
Ojerogwe Atwol	5802	Pte.	1st/4th Bn. K.A.R.	E. Africa	14 Jan. 1918
West African Native Personnel					
Awudu Illo	5992	Pte.	3rd Bn. Nigeria R.	E. Africa	18 Jun. 1917
Chinese Personnel					
Chao Wen Te	30828	Coolie	57 (Chinese) Coy., Lab. Corps	France	1 Apr. 1920
Liu Dien Chen		1st Cl. Ganger	108 (Chinese) Coy., Lab. Corps	France	1 Apr. 1920
Wang Chen Ching	30064	Labourer	57 (Chinese) Coy., Lab. Corps	France	1 Apr. 1920
Wang Yu Bhan	15333	Labourer	59 (Chinese) Coy., Lab. Corps	France	22 Nov. 1919
Yen Teng Feng	91085	1st Cl. Ganger	130 (Chinese) Coy., Lab. Corps	France	13 Jul. 1920

["On 23rd May 1919 at Bailleul following an explosion, he worked constantly for four hours removing tarpaulins from stacks of ammunition and drenching them with water."]

NOTES

1. Pte. E. Airlie, S.-Sgt. G. J. Bakewell and Cpl. A. J. Carnell, all 89 Coy., R.A.O.C. in same list of awards.
2. An official record exists of a recommendation for Private T. Aldrew, 5th Bn. E. Lancs. R. and Private J. Etchell, 3rd/9th Bn. Manchester R. in the following terms:

   "At an inquest held on 13th May 1916 into the circumstances attending the death of an employee of the British Explosive Syndicate Ltd., the coroner was desired by the jury to express their high appreciation of the services rendered by Privates Aldrew and Etchell and the hope that their action might be suitably recognised.
   Both men, at very great risk, entered the heat testing room which had been set on fire owing to an explosion of nitro-glycerine, and were successful in recovering the heat tester, who, however, succumbed later to the injuries he had received."

   In view of the similarity of the names, this recommendation probably refers to the awards to Private E. B. Aldren and Private J. Etchells, though it is curious that their awards appear in different gazettes.
3. L.-Sgt. N. Allport, L.-Cpl. A. Gauld and L.-Cpl. J. W. Scott, all 4th Bn. North'd Fus. in same list of awards.
4. Awarded for services following the disaster at the Explosive Loading Company's works at Faversham, Kent on 2nd April 1916. For full account see *Journal of the Orders and Medals Research Society*, Summer 1979.
5. Gnr. C. Baynton and Dvr. W. M. Hurst, both London Div. Amn. Col., R.F.A. in same list of awards.
6. Pte. A. W. W. Biddlecombe and Pte. F. W. G. Gollop, both 2nd Bn. Dorset R. in same list with joint citation.
7. Bdr. H. Biggs, Dvr. D. R. Thomas and Farr. S.-Sgt. Z. Woolridge, all 8 Div. Amn. Col., R.F.A. in same list of awards.
8. An official record exists of a recommendation dated November 1915 for award of the Albert Medal to Lieut. A. Deschamps-Woolard and L.-Cpl. A. C. Bird, both A.S.C., in the following terms:

   "During a fire at a depot in France Lieutenant A. Deschamps-Woolard, assisted by Lance-Corporal Bird, at considerable personal risk climbed a ladder resting on a lean-to spanning the canal adjoining the burning building. The former, with the aid of a large wall bolt which was luckily to hand, succeeded in smashing the iron frame of the window and extricating a Frenchman who was suffering from the effects of smoke and dust and was badly cut."

   The rescue was not assessed as meriting the Albert Medal and the Silver Medal of the Society for the Protection of Life from Fire was awarded to both men. Permission to wear this medal in uniform was refused. It is probable that the award

to L.-Cpl. A. C. Bird gazetted on 21st August 1917 is in belated recognition of the same action, although Lieut. Deschamps-Woolard received no official award.
9. Pte. F. Brannan, Pte. R. Davie and L.-Cpl. G. Derrick, all 104 Coy., M.G. Corps in same list of awards.
10. Pte. A. Brennan, Cpl. D. Ewart and Sgt. J. Maybank, all 761 Area Empl. Coy., Lab. Corps in same list of awards.
11. Sgt. V. Broadhurst, Sgt. J. W. Loosemoore and Sgt. H. G. White, all "P" Special Coy., R.E. in same list of awards.
12. Pte. J. Brockless, Pte. E. Iredale, Pte. W. Jackson and Pte. J. Sidebottom, all H.S. *Oxfordshire* in same list with joint citation.
13. Sgt. L. A. W. Brooks and Spr. S. F. Tobitt, both Rly. Opg. Div., R.E. in same list of awards.
14. Spr. W. J. Cairns, Spr. C. F. Hobbs and Spr. H. Maxfield, all E.M.M.B. Coy., Austr. Engrs. in same list of awards.
15. Bar awarded for a second act of gallantry, see page 25.
16. 2nd Cl. A.M. T. J. Carmody, Sgt. A. G. Dalzell, 1st Cl. A.M. C. M. T. Lee and 1st Cl. A.M. V. Smith, all 69 Squadron Austr. F.C. in same list with joint recommendation.
17. Pte. L. Carr and L.-Cpl. H. E. Sancto, both 1st/1st North'n Fd. Amb., R.A.M.C. in same list of awards.
18. Spr. C. H. Catherall and Spr. T. Simons, both I.W.D., R.E. in same list of awards.
19. Pte. F. R. Catherwood and Pte. A. E. Guyatt, both 4 Austr. Div. Salvage Coy. in same list of awards.
20. 2nd Cpl. W. W. Chapman and Spr. A. G. Robertson, both 18 Lt. Rly. Opg. Coy., R.E. in same list of awards.
21. Spr. F. J. Clayton, L.-Cpl. W. Ford, Spr. H. Gore, L.-Cpl. J. Goulding, Spr. N. Liles, Spr. C. O'Brien and Cpl. A. Robson, all 54 Lt. Rly. Opg. Coy., R.E. in same list of awards.
22. C.Q.M.S. W. J. Clements, C.S.M. E. Read and Cpl. C. E. Voysey, all 11 Pontoon Park, A.S.C. in same list of awards.
23. Duplicate award gazetted 22 November 1919 cancelled 11th February 1920.
24. L.-Bdr. F. Dickens, 545 Siege Bty., R.G.A. and Sgt. P. C. Goodwin, R.A.S.C. (M.T.) att'd 545 Siege Bty., R.G.A. in same list of awards.
25. C.Q.M.S. J. W. Down, District Staff and Gnr. J. McCafferty and Cpl. W. T. White, 85 Coy., R.G.A. in same list of awards.
26. The Royal Flying Corps was part of the Army until it was absorbed into the Royal Air Force on its formation on 1st April 1918. It is possible that details of the actions for which Army Meritorious Service Medals were awarded to Royal Flying Corps personnel are contained in Air Ministry papers at the Public Record Office (Air 1). These have not been researched for this account.
27. Pte. J. Durie and Pte. G. E. Harper, both 1st/7th Bn. R. Scots in same list of awards.
28. Bar awarded for valuable services, see page 26.
29. Sgt. P. A. England and Pte. A. L. Henry, both 3rd Bn. Br. W. Indies R. in same list of awards.
30. Pte. C. Ephgrave, Pte. A. J. Taylor and Pte. A. Williams, 1st (H.S.) Garr. Bn E. Kent R. and Pte. D. L. Gearing, 7th Bn. R. Fus. in same list of awards with joint recommendation.
31. Cpl. G. W. Ethelston and Pte. W. Riley, 88 Lab. Coy., R.E. in same list of awards. Probably for services during a fire on an ammunition train on 15th June 1917. Lieut. C. H. Wade, 88 Lab. Coy. was awarded the Albert Medal for services at the same incident.

32. Sgt. W. Gallagher and L.-Sgt. W. J. Jewell, both R.A.O.C. in same list with joint citation.
33. Spr. T. H. B. Gollan and Spr. J. C. Underwood, both 2 Tunnelling Coy., Austr. Engrs. in same list of awards.
34. Military Medal gazetted 13th August 1919 cancelled 22nd January 1920.
35. The awards to Hardy, Mill and O'Shea were announced in War Office lists published after 1st April 1918 and presumably relate to actions performed prior to their transfer to the Royal Air Force.
36. C.S.M. H. H. Hockney, Spr. P. L. Jackson, Sgt. S. C. Spence and C.S.M. A. Wallace, all 59 Broad Gauge Opg. Coy., Austr. Engrs. in same list of awards.
37. Spr. R. Holywell and Spr. W. Richardson, both 479 Fd. Coy., R.E. in same list of awards.
38. Pte. G. Hood, Cpl. A. Jaggar and Pte. R. E. Mathery, all 12th Bn. Yorkshire L.I. in same list of awards.
39. Spr. F. Jewitt and Sgt. T. Pow, both I.W.D., R.E. in same list of awards and both for services in Mesopotamia.
40. Sgt. A. M. Jones, Pte. H. V. Stephens and Pte. H. J. Walters, all 25th Bn. R. Welsh Fus. in same list of awards.
41. Cpl. J. R. King, Spr. B. McKenna and Spr. R. Melville, all 13 Lt. Rly. Opg. Coy., Can. Rly. Tps. in same list of awards.
42. Pte. A. Kriehn and Pte. J. Malzer, both Middx. R. att'd 1 Inf. Lab. Coy. in same list of awards.
43. Sub.-Condr. R. W. Lewis and Sgt. A. C. Rodrigues, both Rly. Corps, E. African Force in same list of awards. Duplicate awards to both gazetted 16th July 1918. Cancellation not traced.
44. L.-Cpl. H. Marchington and Sgt. C. E. Wilson, both 1 Tramway Coy., Can. Engrs. in same list of awards.
45. Spr. F. W. Pyke and Spr. H. T. Tinckler, both 5th Bn. Can. Rly. Tps. in same list of awards.
46. Pte. W. Rankin and Pte. P. Ryan, both 6th Bn. Connaught Rgrs. in same list of awards.
47. Sgt. J. E. L. Richardson and Sgt. J. J. Smith, both M.G. Corps (Motor) in same list of awards and both for services in Mesopotamia.
48. Dvr. N. Ridley and Dvr. A. Speedie, both R.A.S.C. (H.T.) att'd 52 Fd. Amb., R.A.M.C. in same list of awards.
49. Army Meritorious Service Medal awarded in list originated under War Office auspices.
50. Meritorious Service Medal for valuable services gazetted 3rd June 1919 cancelled 18th December 1919.
51. Cpl. E. Treadaway and 1st Cl. A.M. C. J. Woodford, both R.F.C. in same list of awards.
52. Award dated 25th February 1918.

PART V

SUMMARY OF AWARDS "FOR GALLANTRY"

London Gazette	United Kingdom	Australia	Canada	New Zealand	Other
12 Mar. 1917	33	1			1
17 Apl. 1917	5		1		
26 Apl. 1917	1		1		
11 May 1917	4	1			
26 May 1917	5	2			
18 Jun. 1917	8				1
9 Jul. 1917	3				
18 Jul. 1917	4	1		3	
28 Jul. 1917	10				
21 Aug. 1917	6	4			
29 Aug. 1917	9				
17 Sep. 1917	8	3	1		
28 Sep. 1917	8				
18 Oct. 1917	1				1
2 Nov. 1917	8	1			
19 Nov. 1917	2				
12 Dec. 1917	8				
17 Dec. 1917	5	1			
Total	128	14	3	3	3
14 Jan. 1918					2
28 Jan. 1918	3				
4 Feb. 1918	1				
23 Feb. 1918	3				
13 Mar. 1918	1				
19 Mar. 1918	8	4		1	
2 Apl. 1918	2		1		
10 Apl. 1918	16	1			
25 Apl. 1918	12				
12 Jun. 1918	10		1		
27 Jun. 1918	1		1		2
16 Jul. 1918	1	1			
6 Aug. 1918	9	2			
29 Aug. 1918	3				
13 Sep. 1918	15	1			
7 Oct. 1918	12		1		
21 Oct. 1918	3	1	1		
Total	100	10	5	1	4

London Gazette	United Kingdom	Australia	Canada	New Zealand	Other
24 Jan. 1919	19		1		4
14 May 1919	23	1	5		
17 Jun. 1919	21	2	5		
3 Jul. 1919	17		3		
20 Aug. 1919	10				
20 Oct. 1919	19	1			
22 Nov. 1919	4				1
18 Dec. 1919	4				2
Total	117	4	14	–	7
15 Jan. 1920	1				
22 Jan. 1920	1				
11 Feb. 1920			1		
22 Mar. 1920	1				
1 Apl. 1920					3
13 Jul. 1920	1		1		1
17 Sep. 1920	1				
25 Mar. 1921	4		1		
29 Jul. 1921	1				
18 Sep. 1921	1				
11 Jul. 1924	1				
25 Feb. 1927	1				
27 May 1927					2
Total	13	–	3	–	6

Totals

1917	151	128	14	3	3	3
1918	120	100	10	5	1	4
1919	142	117	4	14	–	7
1920–27	22	13	–	3	–	6
	435	358	28	25	4	20

PART VI

AWARDS "FOR DEVOTION TO DUTY"

London Gazette 6th September 1918

"for devotion to duty on the occasion of the sinking or damage by enemy action of hospital ships, transports or store ships."

All these recipients of the Meritorious Service Medal were also mentioned in despatches in the *London Gazette* of 6th September 1918, which also announced awards of the D.S.O., M.C. and R.R.C. and additional mentions.

BENNETT	310446	Pte. A.	JONES	310196	F.Q.M.S. J. W.
BIDDELLS	310022	L.-Cpl. G.	NEWMAN	311302	S.-S.Cpl. J.
BOWEN	310010	Pte. A. J.	PEARSON	310255	Sgt. J. E.
COLLEY	310725	Sgt. C. H.	SPENCER	310307	Pte. J. J. H.
COX	1468	Sgt. E. J. (died)	TRENFIELD	310458	Cpl. E. G.
DAULMAN	310106	L.-Cpl. H. H.	WARNER	310354	Pte. T.
DIXON	310104	Pte. J.	WILKES	2184	L.-Cpl. J. A.
FARNDON	310120	Pte. F.	WOODWARD	310406	Pte. A.
HOUGH	310181	Sgt. B., M.M.	YOUNG	2119	Pte. H. M.

All 1st/1st Warwickshire Yeomanry (Pte. Young gazetted as 285970, Oxfordshire Hussars).

[On 10th April 1915 over 750 horses and mules of 1st/1st Warwickshire Yeomanry with a strong detachment from the regiment sailed from Avonmouth in the Hired Transport *Wayfarer*. The ship was torpedoed on 11th April and abandoned, passengers and crew being rescued by S.S. *Framfield*. As *Wayfarer* did not sink, the officer in command, Major R. A. Richardson, called for volunteers to go back on board to look after the horses while the ship was towed into Queenstown. As a result of the efforts of this party of two officers and eighteen other ranks all the animals were brought safely ashore after a two-day tow in rough weather. The whole party was mentioned in despatches, two officers received the Military Cross and the eighteen other ranks listed here, the Meritorious Service Medal. (See *The Warwickshire Yeomanry in the Great War*.)]

ATKINSON	51307	L.-Cpl. C.	HOGAN	31764	S.M. J. E.
BAIDEN	19202	S.M. F. J. R.	LEYSHON	49292	Pte. W.
BROWNLOW	7195	L.-Cpl. T.	MCCORMACK	35076	Sgt. E. H.
DARWEN	1742	Cpl. I.	MCGUIRE	51140	Sgt. J.
HANRAHEN	19805	S.M. J.	VEINO	53649	Pte. L.

All R.A.M.C.

London Gazette 29th September 1919

"for devotion to duty during an epidemic in a prisoner of war camp, Germany."

BANNIGAN	2128	R.S.M. J. F. M.	2nd. Bde., Austr. F.A.
WOOD	1466	Pte. R.	2nd Bn. Austr. M.G. Corps.
WORSFOLD	6/SR/6987	Pte. F. J.	1st Bn. Middx. R.

London Gazette 28th November 1919

"in recognition of their exceptional devotion in the performance of military duties."

CARROLL	453948	Pte. J. F.	11th Bn. London R.
FIDDES	275258	Sgt. A. F., D.C.M., M.M.	6th Bn. Essex R.
JONES	27960	L.-Cpl. R. C.	1st Bn. Leinster R.
LAWTON	TT/02450	Sgt. R. G.	R.A.V.C.
REYNOLDS	277612	Sgt. G. N.	6th Bn. Essex R.

London Gazette 3rd January 1920

"for devotion to duty with the British Forces in Siberia."

DE RAMER	WR/208613	R.S.M. F.	R.E.
HAWKINS	479168	S.M.I. B. H.	R. Can. R.
HUBBARD	479141	S.M.I. E.	R. Can. R.
IVENS	WR/210329	Spr. T. E.	R.E.
SMITH	479176	S.M.I. E. H.	R. Can. R.
TOVEY	WR/208306	Sgt. G.	R.E.
WALTERS	WR/200257	C.S.M. F. I.	R.E.
WHITE	479148	S.M.I. F.	R. Can. R.

London Gazette 30th January 1920

"in recognition of devotion to duty and valuable services rendered whilst prisoners of war or interned." [Awards dated 5th May 1919]

ALLENBY	5352	Pte. E.	R.A.M.C.
ANDREWS	8288	S.M. M.	R.A.M.C.
ANDREWS	10733	Pte. T.	1st Bn. R. Lancaster R.
AUSTIN	10871	Pte. H.	1st Bn. Loyal R.
BABISTER	70149	Sgt. W. J.	1st/1st Berks. Yeo.
BATT	12927	L.-Cpl. W.	4th Bn. R. Fus.
BELL	8506	Pte. W. J.	1st Bn. R. Scots Fus.
BATEMAN	7687	Pte. W.	2nd Bn. W. Riding R.
BISHOP	3/6520	L.-Cpl. J. W.	1st Bn. Dorset R.
BISHOP	50620	Gnr. S.	R.F.A.
BOARDMAN	14523	Cpl. W.	4th Bn. R. Fus.
BOOK	8081	Pte. T. E.	1st Bn. Northants. R.
BOON	10464	C.Q.M.S. W., M.M.	2nd Bn. R. Dublin Fus.

BOYCE	8276	Sgt. A. H.	2nd Bn. Yorkshire L.I.
BRAMLEY	10204	Pte. J.	4th Bn. R. Fus.
BRASHAW	9219	Sgt. F. J.	1st Bn. Cheshire R.
BRAZEAR	L/9789	Pte. W.	4th Bn. Middx. R.
BRISTOW	11151	Pte. W.	4th Bn. R. Fus.
BUMPSTEAD	109247	R.S.M. R.	4th Bn. Can. Mtd. Rifles
BURGESS	M2/082579	Pte. H. G.	R.A.S.C.
BYNG	550364	Pte. N. C.	16th Bn. London R.
CASH	2875	Pte. J. R.	19th Austr. Inf. Bn.
CHARTER	7005	Pte. E.	1st Bn. Hampshire R.
CHATFIELD	7695	Pte. R.	1st Bn. Cheshire R.
CHECKETTS	9363	Pte. H. J. F.	1st Bn. R. Berks. R.
CLEE	9308	Pte. J. T.	1st Bn. S. Staffs. R.
CONSTABLE	16224	Pte. G., M.M.	R.A.M.C.
COOK	6749	B.S.M. W.	R.G.A.
COOPER	35669	Gnr. E.	R.G.A.
COURTMAN	7372	Pte. J.	1st Bn. Scots Gds.
DAVIS	9043	Pte. H. V.	2nd Bn. Yorkshire L.I.
DELARA	3865	R.S.M. G., D.C.M.	2nd Bn. Dorset R.
DOLPHIN	10393	L.-Cpl. J.	1st Bn. R. Welsh Fus.
DOLTON	1882	Pte. A.	4th Bn. R. Fus.
DUNN	441	Pte. J.	1st Bn. Coldstream Gds.
FAULKNER	87	Pte. C.	1st Bn. Gordon Highrs.
FELSTEAD	2178	Pte. H. E., M.M.	R.A.M.C.
FRANCIS	7278	R.Q.M.S. W. A.	1st Bn. Cheshire R.
FRENCH	5747	Pte. W. H.	1st Bn. Scots Gds.
FROGGATT	8734	C.Q.M.S. H.	1st Bn. Gordon Highrs.
GARDENER	9645	Pte. G. E.	1st Bn. Ox. and Bucks. L.I.
GARRATT	7648	Pte. W.	1st Bn. Cheshire R.
GERRARD	1642	Pte. G. C.	1st Bn. Loyal R.
GIBB	6826	C.S.M. A.	2nd Bn. A. and S. Highrs.
GOODERHAM	10561	Pte. W. J.	2nd Bn. W. Riding R.
GOODMAN	10310	Cpl. W. T.	1st Bn. R. Welsh Fus.
GOUDE	550076	Pte. H. F.	16th Bn. London R.
GOULDER	9111	Pte. F. G.	1st Bn. R. Scots Fus.
HANCKEL	7007	L.-Cpl. F. C.	13th Austr. Inf. Bn.
HAMILTON	5330	R.S.M. H.	2nd Bn. R. Irish Fus.
HARNETT	D/20021	S.Q.M.S. W.	4th D.G.
HARRISON	8858	Pte. F. A.	1st Bn. North'd Fus.
HEANEY	8481	Pte. J.	R. Inniskilling Fus.
HEATLEY	40566	Sgt. R.	2nd Bn. Lancs. Fus.
HUGHES	341393	Pte. J.	R.A.M.C.
ISHERWOOD	3/1242	L.-Cpl. M.	1st Bn. Loyal R.
JEFFERY	7504	Sgt. H. J.	1st Bn. Hampshire R.
JESSIMAN	9907	Sgt. W.	1st Bn. Gordon Highrs.
KELLET	10366	Pte. S.	2nd Bn. W. Riding R.
MCALISTER	10670	Pte. A.	1st Bn. Gordon Highrs.

Name	Number	Rank	Unit
McDavid	359091	Pte. H. G.	6th Bn. L'pool R.
McIntyre	9635	Pte. L.	3rd Bn. Can. Inf.
MacIntyre	1425	Cpl. D.	1st Bn. Gordon Highrs.
McKenzie	11688	Pte. J. M.	1st Bn. H.L.I.
McLaren	422	Pte. A.	1st Bn. Gordon Highrs.
McLeod	11656	Pte. N.	1st Bn. H.L.I.
Manser	7226	Pte. W. M.	1st Bn. Scots Gds.
Mappley	230126	Sgt. P.	2nd Bn. London R.
Mather	4081	Pte. R.	1st Bn. Loyal R.
Melvin	9156	Pte. W.	2nd Bn. R. Scots
Messam	10420	L.-Cpl. G.	1st Bn. H.L.I.
Miller	6579	Pte. J.	1st Bn. R. Scots Fus.
Mitten	108393	Cpl. H. M.	1st Bn. Can. Mtd. Rifles
Molloy	11026	Pte. R.	1st Bn. Loyal R.
Niell	9052	L.-Cpl. G. R.	2nd Bn. W. Riding R.
Nixon	8686	Pte. F.	1st Bn. Cheshire R.
Parkinson	7579	Pte. F. T.	2nd Bn. Scots Gds.
Paterson	7140	Pte. W.	1st Bn. Cameron Highrs.
Peacock	9282	Sgt. E. T.	4th Bn. Worcs. R.
Pears	6090	Pte. G.	2nd Bn. R. Warwicks R.
Peet	390428	L.-Cpl. D. W.	9th Bn. London R.
Perkins	6389	Pte. B. F. J.	1st Bn. Cameron Highrs.
Phelps	510101	Pte. H. C.	14th Bn. London R.
Pickles	M2/032754	Pte. A.	R.A.S.C.
Pointon	6648	Pte. W. S.	1st Bn. Cheshire R.
Prosser	66292	Bdr. T.	82 Bty., R.F.A.
Punton	5500	Pte. E.	1st Bn. Scots Gds.
Purser	27008	Cpl. H. M.	15th Bn. Can. Inf.
Rawlings	890	Pte. A. J.	2nd Austr. Inf. Bn.
Read	4450	R.S.M. W. A.	2nd Bn. Suffolk R.
Reid	972	Pte. W.	1st Bn. Gordon Highrs.
Roberts	67734	Dvr. G. E.	R.F.A.
Roberts	9939	Pte. J. T. V.	2nd Bn. W. Riding R.
Robertson	10024	Sgt. J.	1st Bn. Gordon Highrs.
Rose	9321	Pte. W.	2nd Bn. K.R.R.C.
Sayers	72720	Pte. C. F. W.	R.A.M.C.
Scott	9161	Pte. R.	1st Bn. Cameron Highrs.
Shambrook	10560	Pte. T. A. E.	1st Bn. Loyal R.
Shepherd	6031	Pte. J.	1st Bn. Cheshire R.
Sidwell	L/13757	Pte. F. E.	4th Bn. Middx. R.
Spence	2880	Cpl. A.	2nd Bn. Scots Gds.
Stiff	8176	Pte. A. J.	1st Bn. Lincoln R.
Taylor	9105	Pte. J.	2nd Bn. R. Irish R.
Tew	11917	Pte. E. J.	1st Bn. H.L.I.
Toon	255097	Cpl. E.	Leics. Yeo.
Turner	21210	Pte. H. J. J.	2nd Bn. Bedfs. and Herts. R.
Walsh	9958	Pte. J.	2nd Bn. S. Lancs. R.
Want	6510	R.S.M. A.	2nd Bn. Cheshire R.

WILLIAMS	7755	L.-Cpl. T.	1st Bn. Bedfs. and Herts. R.
WOODFORD	26491	Sgt. A. W.	R.H.A.

London Gazette 11th February 1920

"in recognition of his exceptional devotion in the performance of military duty."

McCORMICK	24466	Pte. J.	1st Garr. Bn. Sco. Rifles

London Gazette 29th March 1922

"in recognition of devotion to duty and valuable services rendered while prisoners of war in Eastern Anatolia."

ANKERS	M/24819	L.-Cpl. H. D.	R.A.S.C.
CARTER	7810248	Pte. H.	M. G. Corps.
LEADBEATER	7809427	Pte. R.	M.G. Corps.

PART VII

BIBLIOGRAPHY

War Office (M.S.3.). *A Review of new Orders, Decorations and Gallantry Medals instituted by His Majesty during the war 1914–1920, of changes made in existing Orders, Decorations and Gallantry Medals and of certain privileges accorded to recipients of the same and to recipients of a "Mention in Despatches"*. London H.M.S.O., 1920 (for official use only) [M.o.D. Library].

WILSON, Sir A. and McEWEN, J. H. F. *Gallantry—Its Public Recognition* Oxford, University Press, 1939.

ABBOTT, P. E. and TAMPLIN, J. M. A. *British Gallantry Awards* Enfield, Guiness Superlatives Ltd., 1971.

TAMPLIN, J. M. A. and Others *Various Notes and Articles on the Meritorious Service Medal* Journal of the Orders and Medals Research Society 1973–1975.

Transcripts of Crown-copyright records in the Public Record Office appear by permission of the Controller of H.M. Stationery Office.

www.ingramcontent.com/pod-product-compliance
Lightning Source LLC
Chambersburg PA
CBHW060219050426
42446CB00013B/3116